APR 5 2005

JACK M. WATSON
Dean, College-Conservatory of Music
University of Cincinnati
Advisory Editor to Dodd, Mead & Company

PERSPECTIVES
IN MUSIC THEORY
AN HISTORICAL-ANALYTICAL APPROACH

Paul Cooper

PERSPECTIVES
IN MUSIC THEORY
AN HISTORICAL-ANALYTICAL APPROACH

DODD, MEAD & COMPANY
New York   *1973*

PERSPECTIVES
IN MUSIC THEORY

ISBN: 0-396-06752-2

Library of Congress Catalog Card Number: 72-12026

Printed in the United States of America

CONTENTS

PART III *The Completed Major-Minor System*

EDITOR'S INTRODUCTION

A number of its features combine to make *Perspectives in Music Theory* unique, and, in terms of the objectives of comprehensive musicianship, ideal for a freshman-sophomore music-theory program.

First, and foremost, is its comprehensiveness. Not only does it cover the basic theoretical concepts and techniques of music, but it treats them in historical perspective and, where appropriate, it provides interesting and enlightening illustrations from actual music literature. Also, it relates those illustrations to style and performance practice. Unlike so many theory texts—of yesterday and today—it does not limit itself to the common-practice period. Instead, it presents a theoretical overview, with detailed analyses, of the structure and materials of music (and their stylistic mutations) belonging to the major periods of Western music, including the twentieth century. Its analytical concern with the craft of composition extends to tonal texture, orchestration, and the idiomatic use of instruments. While its chief emphases are theoretical and compositional, the text introduces students to an enormous amount of music literature.

Second, notwithstanding its wide coverage of music literature, *Perspectives* is surprisingly concise. Through careful selection and structuring, Dr. Cooper has avoided the error of many writers of books on theory, harmony, counterpoint, form and analysis, and orchestration—the obsession with rules and more rules and even rules about breaking rules. By combining and interrelating the major elements of music theory, he has achieved what *Gestalt* psychologists call "the good *Gestalt*."

Third, *Perspectives* is not biased for or against any specific fields of musical study. Composition majors will find it filled with perceptive information about the craft they are beginning to learn; history and theory majors will find just as perceptive information about musical analysis and approaches to analysis; performance majors will gain insight into the interrelations of analysis, composition, and performance; music education majors will develop skill in explaining and verbalizing about music. This does not mean to imply mutual exclusiveness; quite to the contrary, these various emphases add up to increased comprehensive musicianship.

Fourth, the text is flexible and developed in a manner to lend itself to a variety of approaches. At the University of Cincinnati, for example, it is taught concurrently with a parallel course in music literature.

Fifth, it is grounded on a sound organization and on sound learning principles: the spiral approach provides for progressively deepening students' insight into the complexities of concepts and techniques. The inductive approach (presenting techniques and concepts through actual musical examples) aids recall, adds the essential aural dimension, and makes materials and structures more interesting and meaningful. The principle of motivation is used in a variety of ingenious ways from the beginning to the end of the text—students are encouraged to carry on research, to compose, to prepare verbal and musical analyses, to explore different methods of analysis, and to trace concept and technique mutations through the various style periods.

Sixth, and most basic of all, *Perspectives* works. Five years of testing— with hundreds of students and employing rigorous criteria and objective controls—have proved it.

JACK M. WATSON

PREFACE

Perspectives in Music Theory is designed to be used in the initial two-year sequence at the college level and is written with specific goals in mind. Among these is an expanded historical perspective—musical examples are drawn from about 800 to 1950. It is hoped that by providing the student with a diversity of examples by major composers, he can be encouraged to make intellectual and creative responses imitatively. A further aim is to present concepts which relate to melodic, rhythmic, textural, contrapuntal, and architectural factors—as well as those which pertain to harmonic systems.

The *Perspectives* attempt to be neither so all-inclusive as to eliminate incentive and flexibility for the teacher, nor so skeletal as to require exhaustive explanation for the student. Teacher and student are expected to work as a team, and the text deliberately leaves room for amplification. Further, it veers from the more common approach in that many concepts are discussed several times—with additional information or perspective supplied on each successive occasion, as the need develops. This pedagogical procedure may, at first, be disturbing to the teacher; however, it is better adapted to the learning process than is the limiting of discussion of important concepts to one specific chapter of a text.

Another feature of the text is that "exercises" have been replaced by Suggested Studies, including suggestions for the writing of whole short compositions, with the strongest recommendation for their performance in the classroom. The Suggested Studies also include analytical problems and topics for verbal or expository discussion. This departure from the usual format is based on the assumptions that the competent and imaginative teacher will wish to devise additional assignments, and that the text will be used in conjunction with other materials. In trial use in the classroom the following complements have proven most effective: a programmed fundamentals outline in book form, an aural program, a separate sight-singing collection, and an omnibus of musical examples. (The identical omnibus was also employed in the separate but correlated music literature lectures and recitations.)

Part I is concerned primarily with theoretical concepts. The brief discussions of counterpoint, instruments, musical form, etc., are pedagogically calculated as introductions; they are certainly not intended as substitutes for thorough study. Rather, these materials are presented because in most music schools specific courses in these subjects are not elected until the junior or senior year—a late point, in my opinion, at which to begin thinking about the "color of melody," the "form of harmony," and such other important aspects of music as texture, fabric, environment, musical event and non-event. Part II examines "familiar-style" (chordal) excerpts and short compositions from the Renaissance and early Baroque periods. These discussions and analyses are preceded by brief introductions of Medieval sacred and secular examples. Parts III and IV respond to the periods of 1650 to 1890 and 1890 to 1950 respectively, with examples drawn from varied media.

In a manner of speaking, most college texts are written by students. The debt I owe my students is profound. I am grateful also to my colleagues at the University of Michigan, where these ideas were initially tested, for their encouragement and advice: to Professors Wallace Berry, Edward Chudacoff, and John Lowell; to Paul Boylan and George Burt, whose suggestions and examination, through brilliant teaching, were of the greatest inspiration; to Jerry Dean, Tom Harris, Richard McGowan, George Parrish, and other teaching assistants who presented these materials; similarly, to Robert Elam, John Larkin, Ellsworth Milburn, and James Riley of the University of Cincinnati, where the text was subsequently used and completed, for their recommendations and support; and to Dr. Edith Borroff of Eastern Michigan University, for her sage counsel.

PAUL COOPER

PART I

Theoretical Concepts

"If you would understand the invisible, look carefully at the visible."

—*from the Talmud*

1

MUSICAL THEORY

MUSICAL AESTHETICS

**MUSICAL
THEORY**

Music is the art and science of organized sound. Its existence is noted in every major culture; its origin as an accompaniment to ritual predates science. Music (Gk., *mousikē tekhnē*, Muses' art) may have a special significance according to time or place: "Music is the arithmetic of sound" is attributed to the Germans, while "Music is an emotion whose poetry is but high philosophy" is purportedly Italian; seemingly the French have countered with "Music is the most expensive of all noises."

Theory is the body of fundamental principles underlying a science or an application of science. Thus *musical theory* encompasses the classified study of rhythm, melody, harmony, solfege, counterpoint, form, orchestration. It also embraces acoustics, calculations of intervals, scales, harmonic composites on the scientific side, and aesthetics as a speculative counterpart.

Purpose

The study of musical theory should provide the information and the incentive for applying the principles of music to the composition, performance, and historical study of the art. The development of fluent skills in notation and writing, aural-visual analysis, sight-singing and sight-reading, aural perception, and oral and expository articulation are basic and minimum goals to be attained. Theoretical studies should also assist an understanding of the development of Western music—from its sacred and secular origins to contemporary thought and practice. Theory guides the composer in the control of sound and design; it prompts the performer in the creation of sound—from the control of a specific note, through the subtleties of coloring and phrasing, to the realization of an architectural whole; finally, it provides a basis for most serious research into the discipline of music. For all of these reasons theory should be considered the core of study

3

from which are derived the inspiration and knowledge for a continuing comprehensive and creative musicianship.

**MUSICAL
AESTHETICS**

How may one define beauty? When does craft become art? What constitutes a musical masterpiece? These questions have prompted serious dialogue for centuries, and the arguments continue. *Aesthetics* (Gk. *aisthesis*, feeling, sensation) is generally understood as the philosophy or study of the beautiful. Among aestheticians, there are two principal views of music which have prompted these hundreds of years of discourse. In briefest form, these views are: (1) that music is an *heteronomous* art and is capable of expressing extra-musical elements, and (2) that music is an *autonomous* art and may realize only intrinsic principles and ideas.

In the sixth century B.C., Pythagoras commented that music was an expression of universal harmony, which is also realized in mathematics and astronomy. Plato, about 400 B.C., concluded that music was a most appropriate conveyer of social and political education. The great Roman statesman and philosopher Boethius (died A.D. 524) made three divisions of music:

Musica mundana (the Pythagorean harmony of the universe)
Musica humana (the harmony of the soul and body)
Musica instrumentalis (music as actual sound)

About 1619, Kepler correlated musical tones and intervals with the movements of the planets and their astrological functions; two hundred years later, Schopenhauer countered by speculating that "music is the purest incarnation of the absolute will and the expression of human feelings in their abstract interpretation of metaphysical ideas."

At various times music has been thought of as an oratorical art, as a poetry of lesser clarity, as form moving in sounds. There is no one prevailing view of music in the mid-twentieth century; rather, since 1950, the function and very purpose of the art form have been subjected to considerable scrutiny.

**SUGGESTED
STUDIES**

1. Briefly discuss one or more of the following (or similar) topics: "The value of art music versus folk music," "Music as a utilitarian function," "Music as entertainment," "Music as a religion" (in the Wagnerian sense), "Music as an extension of reality."

2. Suggested readings:
   Suzanne Langer, *Philosophy in a New Key* (New York: Mentor, 1948).
   Apel, Willi, ed., *Harvard Dictionary of Music*, "*Aesthetics of Music.*"

2

ACOUSTICAL AND PHYSICAL
PROPERTIES OF SOUND
HARMONIC SERIES
ELEMENTS OF MUSIC
TEMPO AND DYNAMICS

ACOUSTICAL AND PHYSICAL PROPERTIES OF SOUND

The basic materials of music are time and sound. *Time* provides the outer and inner dimensions of organized musical events. *Sound* is the phenomenon which is treated in an elaborate science called *acoustics*. This science is typically divided into four categories:

1. The nature of sound
2. Pitch calculations
3. The study of consonance, dissonance, and resonance
4. Architectural acoustics

Of these, only items 1, 2, and 3 are of immediate concern. As a kind of parenthesis to this discussion it may be observed that in their non-technical meaning, the terms *consonance* and *dissonance* have relative rather than absolute connotations. Some intervals which we deem "consonant" today were heard as "dissonances" in Medieval times. Similarly, observe that the same chord (X) in Example 1 might be considered either consonant or dissonant, depending on its context, behavior, and dynamic relation.

Example 1

a. Chord X is relatively "consonant"
b. Chord X is relatively "dissonant"

Frequency

Frequency refers to the number of vibrations per second effected by an elastic body when the equilibrium of this body is in some way disturbed. *Pitch*, a subjective synonym, depends upon the frequency of vibration for its specific designation.

Example 2

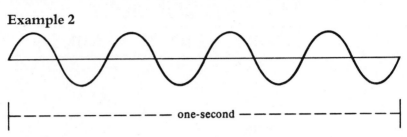

one-second

Amplitude

Amplitude is the amount of energy effecting the vibrational disturbance. It is the measurement of intensity, i.e., soft or loud.

Example 3

Timbre

Timbre is the quality or color of a sound. The timbre of a given tone is determined by the number and relative intensity of its *overtones*.

**HARMONIC
SERIES
(Overtone Series)**

A single note consists of a *fundamental* and an additional complex of sound called the natural *harmonic series*[1] or *overtone series*. The overtone series is of great interest for both practical and historical reasons. All wind instruments are played in accordance with the series; similarly, natural harmonics on string instruments are overtone resultants.

Example 4

Both in vocal and in instrumental music, chordal formations typically take advantage of the natural phenomenon of the overtone series.

---

[1] The term *partials* has a similar meaning to "harmonics" and "overtones." For proper distinction, however, the fundamental is included in the calculation of partials, excluded for calculations of harmonics and overtones.

Example 5

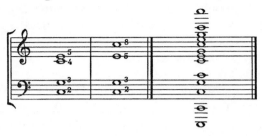

a. Chordal formations   **b.** An orchestral sonority

Interestingly, the structure of the overtone series coincides, in a very general way, with the development of Western music:

1. Unison singing or the singing in octaves (magadizing) in Greek music and in Ambrosian and Gregorian chant.
2. Organum (motion in parallel fourths and fifths); from c. 850. Organum is generally considered to be the origin of polyphony (see p. 8).
3. Triadic music; from c. 1400.
4. Addition of the chordal seventh (C E G B♭); from c. 1600.
5. Addition of the chordal ninth (C E G B♭ D); from c. 1750.
6. Use of the whole-tone scale (B♭ C D E F♯); from c. 1880.
7. Total chromaticism and the twelve-tone technique, as well as experimentation with microtones, emerging in the first part of this century.

ELEMENTS OF MUSIC

The *elements* of music refer to the broad components: rhythm, melody, harmony, color, and texture.

Rhythm is a term used to describe the temporal quality (duration) of sound.

Melody is a succession of pitches; by its nature it cannot be separated from rhythm.

Harmony is the resultant of the simultaneous combination of two or more musical sounds.

Color is a term used to identify the quality of sound produced by voices or instruments.

Texture denotes the dispositions of pitch and timbre, as well as the horizontal and vertical dimensions of sound. The term is frequently modified as:

   Monophonic: single-line melody
   Heterophonic: the elaboration, in time, of one melody or harmony

Polyphonic: two or more simultaneous melodic lines. Actually, polyphonic meant *written* as several parts. "Familiar polyphony" was chordal (note for note) as of c. 1470. Today, chordal passages are typically referred to as
Homophonic: chordal

**TEMPO AND
DYNAMICS**

Tempo (L. *tempus*, time) refers to the rate of a given duration: $\quad = 60$, or $\quad = 144$. Typically, composers indicate a general rate or tempo by using Italian or English words such as *adagio* (It., slowly, softly), *allegro* (It., cheerful), *moderately slow*, or *very fast*. Dynamic indications specify sound-volume. Abbreviations of Italian words such as *pianissimo* (*pp*), *fortissimo* (*ff*), *sforzato* (*sf* or *sfz*), *forte-piano* (*fp*), as well as symbols ⊂ (increasing in volume) and ⊃ (decreasing in volume) are commonly employed.

**SUGGESTED
STUDIES**

1. Memorize the overtone series as presented in Example 4. Write the series from three different fundamentals:
   a. B♭ (a whole step lower)
   b. C♯ (a half step higher)
   c. c♮ (an octave higher)
2. Search for examples of music which are predominantly of one kind of texture: monophonic, heterophonic, polyphonic, or homophonic. Note the period of composition and the composer.
3. Using a music dictionary or encyclopedia, study the *precise* meaning of commonly used Italian terms such as: *prestissimo, con brio, cantabile, andante, largo, lento.*

3

THE NOTATED PAGE

NOTATION

THE NOTATED PAGE The signs, symbols, and words which comprise musical notation have both a specific order and a precise rendering. Observe in Example 6 the placement of the composer's name, the poet's name, and the title. The English translations and the composer's dates are obvious editorial additions.

Example 6

AM LEUCHTENDEN SOMMERMORGEN
On a Shining Summer Morning
(Dichterliebe, Op. 48, 1840)

Heinrich Heine

Robert Schumann
(1810–1856)

Ziemlich langsam

Am leuch - ten-den Som - mer -
On a shin - ing sum - mer

Since the time of Haydn and Mozart, most tempi have been indicated. Dynamics are placed between the staves in keyboard music, below the staff in instrumental music, and above the staff in vocal music. Braces, clefs, key signatures, and meter signatures have a standard and set order. All lines of music which are to be heard simultaneously are connected by a minimum of one vertical bar. An additional brace is employed for the keyboard or for instruments of like or identical quality. A single staff of music (e.g., a work for solo violin) has no initial bar.

Example 7

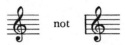

Staff (Stave)

Staff or *stave* refers to the five horizontal lines upon or between which the notes and rests are indicated. In general, notation represents the visual image of sound placement. The invention of the staff (four lines) is credited to Guido d'Arezzo (c. 1000), who recommended that the lines indicate d f a c^i. A five-line staff was used as early as 1200, while the system most commonly used today dates from the late sixteenth century.

Clefs

Clefs indicate the location of a particular pitch. Most common are the treble, or G clefs, and the bass, or F clefs. C clefs, used commonly in earlier music, are retained today for the viola and, on occasion, for the cello, bassoon, and trombone. Although all clefs are moveable, one observes primarily the moveable C clef. Study Example 8 carefully; compare 8c and 8h.

Example 8

a.   b.   c.   **d.** Soprano **e.** Mezzo soprano **f.** Alto **g.** Tenor **h.** Baritone

Fluency in reading clefs is indispensable in the study of orchestral scores and in negotiating transpositions. Example 9 illustrates a simple transposition.

Example 9

a. Original   **b.** Change clefs, key signature   **c.** Resultant sound

Key Signatures

A *key signature* constitutes a pre-inventory of pitches that require either a sharp or a flat; it traditionally indicates one of two keys: the major tonic or the minor tonic.

All signs for signatures and for *accidentals* are derived from a common source—the letter *b*. Its introduction was prompted in part by the avoidance in Medieval music of a particular sonority called the *tritone*.

Example 10

♭ = *molle* (soft) = flat
♮ = *durum* (hard) = natural
♯ = derived from ♮ (hard) = sharp

NOTATION

Notation is a system of signs and symbols to represent the aural realization of music. *Neumes* (Gk. *neuma*, nod, sign) provided a basis for a notational system in the Middle Ages (c. 700 to c. 1300). A few common neumes illustrate this graphic representation:

Neumatic

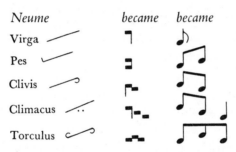

Neume		became	became
Virga			
Pes			
Clivis			
Climacus			
Torculus			

Mensural

Common or standard notation in use today is derived from *mensural notation*, a system established by Franco of Cologne c. 1250. There were two divisions in this system:

Black mensural, from c. 1250 to 1450
White mensural, from c. 1450 to 1600

A table of equivalents shows the relation of mensural to standard notes and rests:

	Maxima	Longa	Brevis	Semibrevis	Minima	Sm[1]	F[2]	Sf[3]
Notes:	⊐	⊐	□	◊	♩	♩ (♪)	♪(♪)	♪
Standard equivalents:			⊧	○	♩	♩ ♪	♪ ♪	♪

From about 1600, and continuing for 350 years, composers pro-

---

[1] Sm = semiminima
[2] F = fusa
[3] Sf = semifusa

vided for the gradual development of the notation system in current
use. Since c. 1950 several new systems have emerged—each attempting
to serve the expressive needs of the composer while solving the
technical problems of the performer. Examples 11 through 14
illustrate that notation has been, and is, a constantly changing process,
appropriate for the particular sound it represents.

Example 11

Neumatic, modern Gregorian; from the *Graduale Vaticanum*

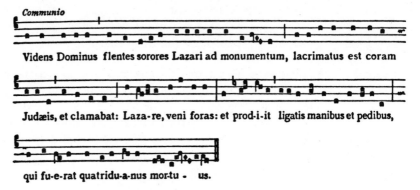

Example 12

White mensural; from *Paragon des Chansons,* printed at Lyons, 1538,
by Jacques Moderne. The example shows the superius and tenor of
a part book. Composed by Pierre Certon.

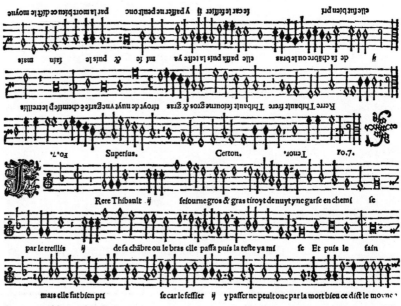

Courtesy of Samuel F. Pogue.

Example 13

Excerpt from *Threnody: To the Victims of Hiroshima*, Krzysztof Penderecki (1933–   )

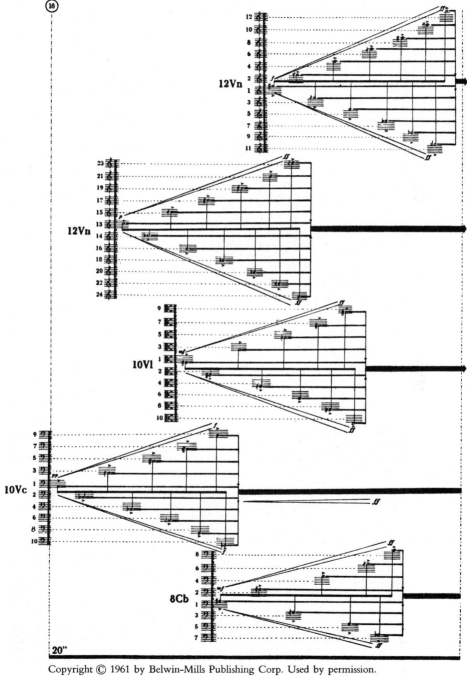

Example 14

Fragment from an electronic score, *Studie II*, Karlheinz Stockhausen
(1928–   )

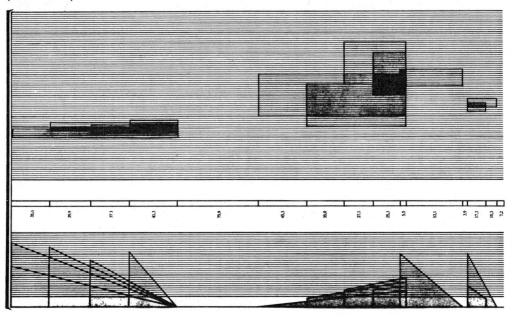

SUGGESTED
STUDIES

1. Study and compare the two notations below. Be able to discuss the similarities and differences between the two versions.

a.

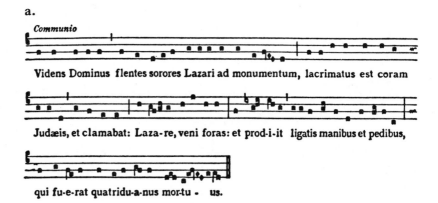

Communio

Videns Dominus flentes sorores Lazari ad monumentum, lacrimatus est coram

Judæis, et clamabat: Laza-re, veni foras: et prod-i-it ligatis manibus et pedibus,

qui fu-e-rat quatridu-a-nus mor-tu - us.

b.

Vi-dens Do-mi-nus flen-tes so-ro-res La-za-ri ad mo-nu-

-men-tum, la-cri-ma-tus est co-ram Ju-dæ-is et cla-ma-bat:

La-za-re, ve-ni fo-ras: et prod-i-it li-ga-tis ma-

-ni-bus et pe-di-bus, qui fu-e-rat qua-tri-du-

-a-nus mor-tu-us.

(When the Lord saw the sisters of Lazarus weeping at the tomb he wept before the Jews, and cried out: 'Lazarus, come forth!' And he who had been four days dead came forth, bound hand and foot.)

The above examples are found in *The New Oxford History of Music* (London: Oxford University Press, 1954), Vol. II, p. 118. Used by permission.

2. Copy about 12 measures of a song or duo of your choice; transpose the selected fragment by using appropriate clefs.

4

OCTAVE IDENTIFICATION

TEMPERAMENT

SCALES

MODES

OCTAVE
IDENTIFICATION
The *octave* is considered the most perfect consonance of all intervals, with a frequency ratio of $1:2$ from any given initial pitch (i.e., if a $=$ 220, then $a^i = 440$, and $a^{ii} = 880$. This relationship is a natural phenomenon which has been referred to as the "basic miracle of music." Its use is common in most music systems. Of several octave designations, the one cited in the table below is commonly employed:

Example 15

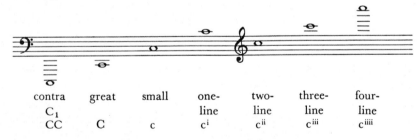

contra	great	small	one-line	two-line	three-line	four-line
C_1						
CC	C	c	c^i	c^{ii}	c^{iii}	c^{iiii}

Other pitches are reckoned *above* the C designations:

Example 16

a^i	D	g^{ii}	A_2 or AAA $8va.$

TEMPERAMENT
Temperament refers to the various tuning systems for the subdivision of the octave. Four principal temperaments have been used in Western music:

16

The *Pythagorean system*, discussed by Pythagoras c. 550 B.C., derives all tones from the interval of the *pure fifth*; e.g., F c g d^i a^i e^{ii}.

Just intonation is a system of tuning in which all intervals are derived from the pure fifth (as in the Pythagorean system) AND the *pure third*.

The *mean-tone system*, in use c. 1500, utilizes a smaller fifth so that a succession of four such fifths results in a pure third; e.g., c g d^i a^i e^{ii} (pure).

Equal temperament, as its name implies, divides the octave into twelve equal parts (semi-tones). Demand for the system grew in the sixteenth century and it came into common use in the early eighteenth century; its universality was not accepted, however, until about 1850. Equal temperament is the basis of most Western music performed or written today.

SCALES

Scale (It. *scala*, ladder) is a term which denotes an ordered arrangement of pitch materials. Strictly interpreted, the term implies a sequence of rising pitches—usually defined within the octave. The basis of traditional Western music is the *diatonic scale* (c d e f g a b c^i), consisting of both whole tones and semi-tones. A scale comprised of only semi-tones results in a *chromatic* or *duodecuple* scale. Most scales consist of five to eight different pitches, with seven tones (heptonic) being the most usual. There is no theoretical preclusion, however, to three–note or eleven-note scales. From the twelve chromatic pitches of the octave, a myriad of scale formations are possible. Ten different scales are shown in Examples 17–19.

Example 17

Very common (the basis of Western music from c. 1600 to 1900):

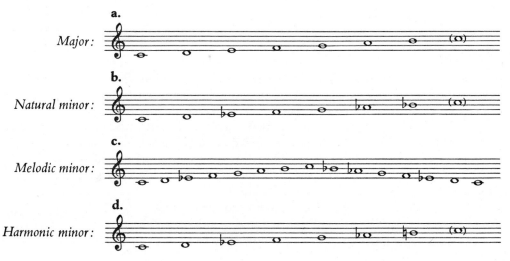

Major:

Natural minor:

Melodic minor:

Harmonic minor:

Example 18

Less common:

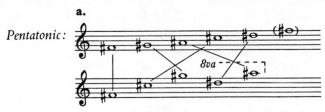

a.

Pentatonic:

Observe that this pentatonic scale may be derived from the projection of equidistant intervals.

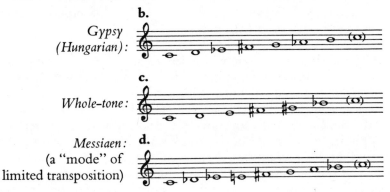

b.

Gypsy
(Hungarian):

c.

Whole-tone:

Messiaen:
(a "mode" of
limited transposition)

d.

Example 19

Other formations:

a.

Invented:

b.

Invented:

MODES

Differentiation is made between scale and *mode*, for classification of particular formations identified with Medieval and Renaissance music. These formations are called *Church modes*. The main period of the modal system (c. 800–1500) relied primarily on the first eight modes (shown below in Example 20), which are related to sacred music. Discussion of the entire twelve modes appeared in the sixteenth century with the publication of Glarean's *Dodekachordon* (1547). Although similar in terminology, there is little correspondence between the Greek modes and the Church modes.

Greek modes resulted from conjunct and disjunct tetrachords (four adjacent notes) in descending pitch order: e′ d c b a g f e. Aristoxenus, in the fourth century B.C., presented a sophisticated description of the three principal types of tetrachords—*enharmonic, chromatic,* and *diatonic*—in his treatise entitled *Harmonics.* Depending upon pitch placement and arrangement of whole tones and semi-tones, Greek modes were considered to have effect on the character, even the morality, of the listener and performer. This view is known as the doctrine of *ethos.*

Church modes may be considered as a classification, in the ninth and tenth centuries, of a vast number of melodies known as *chant* or *plainsong.* Classification of melodies, melodic patterns, and formulae, existing in both notated and aural versions, seems to have been based on the following criteria:

1. The range (*ambitus*) of the chant, which is usually limited to an octave plus one or two additional tones.
2. The concluding tone (*finalis*), which typically produces a conclusive effect and, in a certain sense, a tonal orientation to a specific pitch. (The concept of a *confinalis* as a concluding pitch, usually a perfect fifth higher than the expected *finalis,* is observed both in theory and practice.)
3. The "reciting" tone (*psalmtone* or *dominant*) serves as a further delineation of the characteristics of a specific mode.

Example 20 shows the *finalis, dominant,* and *ambitus* of each of the modes.

Example 20

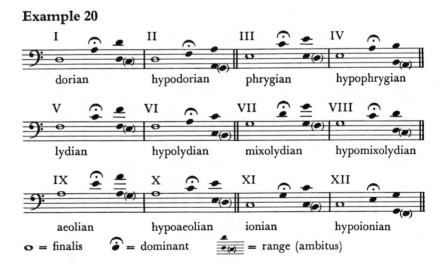

o = finalis   = dominant   = range (ambitus)

Modes I, III, V, VII (IX, XI) are termed *authentic*
Modes II, IV, VI, VIII (X, XII) are called *plagal*
Modes I through VIII remain today as officially designated *Church modes*

Current discussions of modes will include analogies to the keyboard; for example, the observation will be made that dorian includes all the white notes of the keyboard from d to d'. A similar observation suggests that a mode is a specific octave segment of the diatonic (C major) scale with one of the pitches serving as a center tone; that is, *finalis*. Lastly, it is noted that the authentic modes are closely related to the more familiar major and natural minor scales:

Dorian: as natural minor with a raised sixth scale degree
Phrygian: as natural minor with a lowered second scale degree
Lydian: as major with a raised fourth scale degree
Mixolydian: as major with a lowered seventh scale degree

An additional two modes, *locrian* (the white notes from b to b^i) and *hypolocrian*, are theoretically possible but are rarely used. These "hypothetical modes" might be compared to a key signature of ten sharps.

Hexachord

Crucial to the understanding of Medieval and Renaissance music is the concept of *hexachords* (Gk. *hexa*, six; *chordos*, string, tone).

The hexachord of Medieval theory comprised six diatonic tones, with a semi-tone in the middle. There were three such hexachords, as indicated below:

C hexachord, *naturale* (natural): c d e f g a
G hexachord, *durum* (hard): G A B c d e
F hexachord, *molle* (soft): f g a b♭ c^i d^i

By a method of overlapping and the employment of the *free tone* (b-b♭), the "gamut" from great G to e^{ii} was ingeniously spanned.

From Edith Borroff, *Music in Europe and the United States: A History,* © 1971, Prentice Hall, Inc., p. 75.

Tonal

The term *tonal* (with several meanings described later) here refers to music whose melodic and harmonic resources are found in the major and minor scale systems. The impetus toward centripetal (tonal; in a

Twelve-tone

key) theory was derived substantially from Medieval minstrelsy and Renaissance secular composition.

The *twelve-tone* system is primarily a technique of pitch arrangement and utilization devised by Arnold Schoenberg and Josef Hauer in the second decade of this century. The ordering of the twelve pitches contained within the octave may serve as the basis of vertical and horizontal formations in a composition. This set order is called a "row." It should be observed that the row quoted in Example 21 divides into two parts: 1-6 and 7-12, with each part, or hexachord, containing an identical interval makeup.

Example 21

Reprinted from *Edge of Shadow* by Ross Lee Finney (Peters Nr. 6192). © 1960 by Henmar Press, Inc. New York. Reprint permission granted by the publisher.

SUGGESTED
STUDIES

1. Practice identifying any note on the piano by its correct octave name.
2. Examine several pieces of early music for identification of mode.
3. Invent a twelve-tone "row" which divides itself into two parallel hexachords (see Example 21).

5

INTERVALS

TRIADS

KEY SIGNATURES

CADENCES

SOLMIZATION

INTERVALS   The distance between two pitches is called an *interval*. In calculating and describing an interval, at least four different aspects are considered:

1. The theoretical description of consonance or dissonance
2. The arithmetical distance (or difference) between two notes
3. The quality (harmonic color)
4. The indication of whether the interval is contained within an octave (simple) or is greater than an octave (compound)

Consonance, dissonance   Intervals are typically described as being in one of three classes:

Perfect consonants: primes, fourths, fifths, octaves
Imperfect consonants: thirds, sixths (tenths, etc.)
Dissonants: seconds, sevenths (ninths, etc.)

Distance   A facile method of determining *distance* is achieved by the use of a diatonic scale:

Example 22

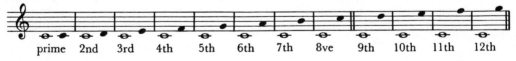

prime   2nd   3rd   4th   5th   6th   7th   8ve   9th   10th   11th   12th

Quality   PERFECT CONSONANTS may be altered to include three forms: perfect, diminished, and augmented. The *decrease* in distance by a semi-tone of a perfect interval results in *diminished* quality; the *increase* in distance by a semi-tone results in *augmented* quality.

Example 23

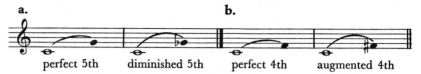

a.   b.

     perfect 5th   diminished 5th   perfect 4th   augmented 4th

IMPERFECT CONSONANTS and DISSONANTS may appear in four forms: augmented, major, minor, and diminished. The *increase* in distance by a semi-tone of a major interval results in *augmented* quality; a semi-tone *decrease* of a major interval results in *minor* quality; a semi-tone *decrease* of a minor interval results in *diminished* quality.

Example 24

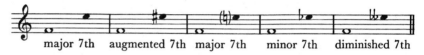

    major 7th   augmented 7th   major 7th   minor 7th   diminished 7th

The intervals produced from the tonic note, ascending in a major scale, are:

> *Perfect:* primes (or unisons), fourths, fifths, octaves
> *Major:* seconds, thirds, sixths, sevenths

A procedural discrepancy occurs in the intervals produced from the tonic note of the natural minor scale. One would assume that this scale would produce perfect and minor intervals; it contains also the *major* second.

> *Perfect:* primes, fourths, fifths, octaves
> *Minor:* thirds, sixths, sevenths
> *Major:* seconds

Simple, compound   Any interval larger than an octave is termed *compound;* those within the octave are called *simple.* Therefore, the total description of the interval in Example 25 is: imperfect consonant, minor tenth, a compound interval.

Example 25

Two observations are in order for intervals of any kind:

1. That the first and last notes are reckoned in determining the distance: C to F is C D E F (= a perfect fourth), NOT D E F . . . as in measuring time.

2. That the arithmetical description remains constant regardless of chromatic alteration or visual appearance on the keyboard. All intervals in Example 26 are sixths:

Example 26

Common abbreviations for the quality of intervals are: P for perfect, A for augmented, M for major, m for minor, d for diminished.

Inversion of intervals

Two principles are essential for determining interval inversion (i.e., c^i *down* to f):

1. The *sum* of the ascending and the descending intervals is 9 (in Example 27, $4 + X = 9$; $X = 5$ or perfect fifth):

Example 27

2. When an interval is inverted, the quality changes for the imperfect consonants and for the dissonants:
   Perfect intervals remain perfect.
   Augmented intervals become diminished.
   Major intervals become minor.
   Minor intervals become major.
   Diminished intervals become augmented.

A few illustrations will clarify these principles:

Example 28

m7 becomes M2   A4 becomes d5   M6 becomes m3

TRIADS

Triad is a term for three tones sounding simultaneously. Four species of triads are the basis of *tertian music;* these species are all derived from positioning a perfect fifth above a given note (see p. 87).

Example 29

Internal coloration results from the use of either a large (major) or small (minor) third. Further modification can be achieved by altering the fifth down a half-step or up a half-step. A facile way of remembering triad quality is shown in Example 30.

Example 30

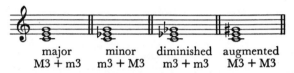

| major | minor | diminished | augmented |
| M3 + m3 | m3 + M3 | m3 + m3 | M3 + M3 |

Triads constructed on each scale degree have a particular nomenclature in tonal music. These names are applicable for any tonic, whether major or minor. Example 31 is constructed in C major.

Example 31

(M)   ii (m)   iii (m)   IV (M)   V (M)   vi (m)   vii° (d)

$$I = tonic$$
$$ii = supertonic$$
$$iii = mediant$$
$$IV = subdominant$$
$$V = dominant$$
$$vi = submediant$$
$$vii° = subtonic \ or \ leading \ tone$$

Observe the relationships and names:
Tonic-mediant-submediant, and
Tonic-dominant-subdominant.

KEY SIGNATURES

Key signatures result from the transposition of the C major scale to any one of the remaining eleven chromatic tones within the octave. In retaining the identical order of whole tones and semi-tones, two "circles of fifths" are effected.

Example 32

Ascending circle:

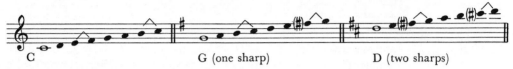

C   G (one sharp)   D (two sharps)

semitones between
       3-4 and 7-8

and continuing UP: A E B F♯ C♯

Example 33

Descending circle:

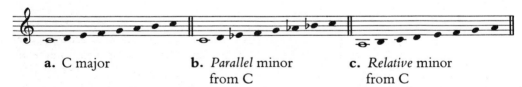

C   F (one flat)   B♭ (two flats)

and continuing DOWN: E♭ A♭ D♭ G♭ C♭

Observe that the two circles produce fifteen different key signatures, of which B-C♭, C♯-D♭, and F♯-G♭ have the same sound *in equal temperament*. These pairs are known as *enharmonic* equivalents.

**Parallel and
relative minor**

      Minor scales are of two categories—*parallel* or *relative*—as determined by their relationship to the major tonic.

Example 34

    a. C major   **b.** *Parallel* minor   **c.** *Relative* minor
                               from C   from C

The relative minor takes the same key signature as major (i.e., two flats for B♭ major or g minor; four sharps for E major or c♯ minor, etc.). The relationship is calculated a minor third *below* the major tonic note. Obviously, the parallel minor signature is derived a minor third *above* the tonic note.
      Semi-tones for the three common minor scales are given below:

Natural minor: 2-3, 5-6
Melodic minor: 2-3, 7-8 ascending; 6-5, 3-2 descending
Harmonic minor: 2-3, 5-6, 7-8

CADENCES

A musical *cadence* (L. *cadere*, to fall) is a temporary or permanent point of repose imposed by any element or combination of elements. For harmonic cadences there are five common types which are cited in Example 35.

Example 35

a.   b.   c.   d.   e.

V   I   V   I   IV   V   IV   I   V   vi

a. *Perfect authentic:* V to I. Both the bass and soprano of the tonic have the chord root.
b. *Imperfect authentic:* V to I. Tonic soprano note is chord third or fifth.
c. *Half* or *semi:* to V. (Normally the dominant is preceded by ii or IV.)
d. *Plagal:* IV to I. This is the familiar "Amen" cadence.
e. *Deceptive:* V to VI is the most typical progression.

SOLMIZATION

Solmization refers to music systems which designate notes by syllable names rather than by letter names. Sight-singing syllables emanated from the *Hymn to St. John*, quoted by Guido d'Arezzo in the eleventh century (see Example 38). The d'Arezzo system involved overlapping hexachords in which the natural (*naturale*), soft (*molle*), and hard (*durum*) hexachords were dovetailed to accommodate an extended range.

Current practice allows for two main systems, *fixed* and *moveable*, with considerable argument among musicians concerning the advantages of each. In the fixed-do system, the syllable name is invariable for any specific note; i.e., all C's (C♯'s, C♭'s), irrespective of tonality or key signature, are called *do* (*ut* in Latin, and retained in French). In the moveable-do system, *do* is always the *tonic* note when in a major key. For a minor key, two possibilities exist: la (tonic) ti do, etc., and do (tonic) re me, etc. The following example illustrates:

Example 36

	Fixed:	re	la	fa	mi	ti (si)	do	re	la	sol	la
	Moveable:	do	sol	mi	re	la	ti	do	sol	fa	sol

The chromatic, or *inflected*, forms of the syllables are cited below:

Example 37

a. Ascending

b. Descending

The *Hymn to St. John* (Example 38), from which the sight-singing syllables were derived, is a most exciting example of subtle musical organization.

Observations:

1. The first note of each of the first six phrases is successively higher (C D E F G A).
2. The seventh phrase (*Sancte Joannes*) responds to gravity and provides a completely satisfying cadence.
3. The melody is *curvilinear* (i.e., exhibits gradually ascending and descending motion); the real high point (*Labii*) is reached at a very specific proportional and mathematical juncture.
4. Three-note cells of varying shape permeate the total time-span.

Example 38

*The seventh syllable, si, was formed from the initials of Sancte Joannes, c. 1650. "That Thy servants may freely sing forth the wonders of Thy deeds, remove all stain of guilt from their unclean lips, O Saint John."

5. The numbers 3 and 7, symbolical and mystical, are to be found at every dimension; for example, there are a total of 49 notes—or seven times seven.
6. Unity and variety are in perfect balance.

SUGGESTED
STUDIES

1. Fluency is essential in the recognition, spelling, and notating of intervals, triads, and key signatures. If these skills have not already been obtained, learn them to the degree of fluency.
2. Analyze any traditional composition for cadence practice.
3. Learn and gain fluency in solmization.
4. Memorize, at the correct pitch level, the *Hymn to St. John.*

6

RHYTHM
CONDUCTING PATTERNS
ACCENTS
RHYTHMIC CONTROLS

RHYTHM

Rhythm denotes the organization of *time* and *duration*. All aspects of temporality relate to one or more of the general classifications of rhythm:

1. *Metrical rhythm:*
   Each time value is a multiple or fraction of a fixed unit (beat). Normal accents recur regularly to provide systematical grouping (measure).
2. *Measured rhythm:*
   Each time value is a multiple or fraction of a specified unit but without regularly recurring accents.
3. *Free rhythm:*
   No common metrical unit is provided.

Metrical rhythm is by far the most common temporal organization in Western music. Metrical schemes are derived from *modal rhythm*, introduced probably by Leoninus shortly before 1200. Briefly, rhythmic modes established the consistent repetition of simple patterns in ternary meter.

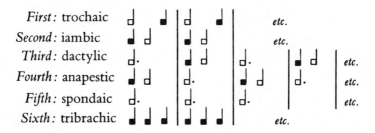

In the early fourteenth century, triple and duple rhythms became

30

coequals—to be followed shortly by dotted rhythms, syncopations, and polyrhythms. The rhythmic complexity of polyphonic music in the late fourteenth century is paralleled only by music written since 1900.

The simplest rhythmic pattern is the alternation of stress and release, or of strong and weak beats. Such a pattern defines *duple* meter (Example 39):

Example 39

It is to be immediately emphasized that this discussion refers to theoretical organization and patterns in time; it is *not* to be construed as a performance ideal. Obviously, the following passage (Example 40) would *not* sound as illustrated—unless specifically so indicated by the composer.

Example 40

Similarly, a pattern consisting of one strong beat followed by two weaker beats is termed *ternary meter* (Example 41):

Example 41

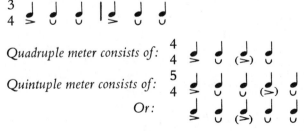

Quadruple meter consists of:

Quintuple meter consists of:

Or:

The terms *simple* and *compound* meters refer to the division of the beats, as illustrated in Example 42:

Example 42

= two subdivisions = *simple*

= three subdivisions = *compound.*

A subdivision which relates to another meter is called a *borrowed division* (Example 43):

Example 43

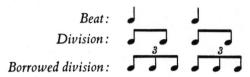

Beat:

Division:

Borrowed division:

The three eighth-notes in the time of two are called a *triplet*. Similar terminology follows in Example 44:

Example 44

4 is a *quadruplet*

5 is a *quintuplet*

6 is a *sextelet*

Frequently used meters with their descriptive names are given below:

Simple duple: $\frac{2}{2} \frac{2}{4} \frac{2}{8} \frac{2}{16}$

Simple triple: $\frac{3}{1} \frac{3}{2} \frac{3}{4} \frac{3}{8} \frac{3}{16} \frac{3}{32}$

Simple quadruple: $\frac{4}{2} \frac{4}{4} \frac{4}{8} \frac{4}{16}$

Simple quintuple: $\frac{5}{2} \frac{5}{4} \frac{5}{8} \frac{5}{16}$

Compound duple: $\frac{6}{2} \frac{6}{4} \frac{6}{8}$

Compound triple: $\frac{9}{2} \frac{9}{4} \frac{9}{8}$

Compound quadruple: $\frac{12}{4} \frac{12}{8} \frac{12}{16}$

Two metrical symbols have survived from mensural notation of the Middle Ages: C and ₵. Initially these symbols referred to *time* (tempus) and *subdivision* (prolatio).

Example 45

	Tempus	Prolatio	Sign	Example	Equivalents
I	Imperfect	Imperfect	C ♌		
II	Perfect	Imperfect	O ♌		
III	Imperfect	Perfect	₵ ♌		
IV	Perfect	Perfect	☉ ♌		

In current practice, the *alla breve* sign (₵), a vestige of mensural proportions, typically signifies the halving of arithmetical ratios, resulting in a different fundamental pulse.

Example 46

C ♩♩♩♩   changing to ₵ ♩♩♩♩

the ♩ becomes the fundamental pulse.

CONDUCTING PATTERNS

Conducting patterns indicate the time and (depending on the tempo) the subdivision (Example 47):

Example 47

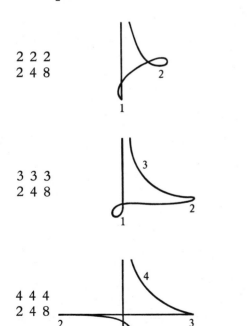

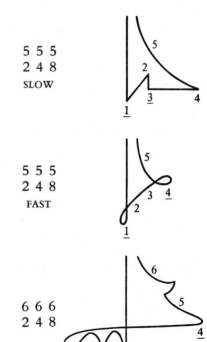

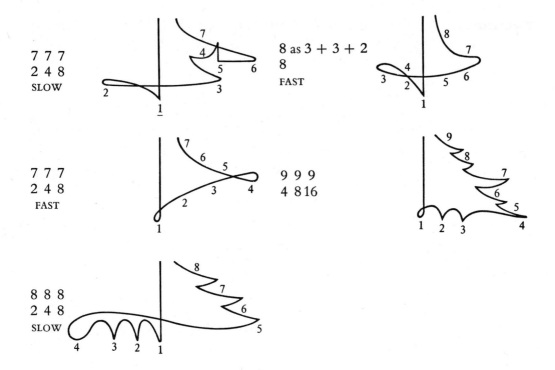

7 7 7
2 4 8
SLOW

8 as 3 + 3 + 2
8
FAST

7 7 7
2 4 8
FAST

9 9 9
4 8 16

8 8 8
2 4 8
SLOW

ACCENTS

Accents are one means of providing for rhythmic vitality. They should be used with great discretion in the performance of music. A thorough knowledge of composer, style, period, and performance practice are essential to the appropriate interpretation of accents. There are three main types of accents which a composer may utilize separately or in combination:

Dynamic accent
Tonic accent
Agogic accent

Dynamic accent

Dynamic accents include the signs and symbols:

$$sf \quad > \quad - \quad \wedge$$

It is understood that, in most music, these signs are within the context of the general dynamic level.

Example 48

Appropriate:
Inappropriate:

Tonic accent

Tonic accent simply refers to a rising pitch. The X notes in Example 49, by their placement and context, are more exposed and noticeable than the other tones in the fragment.

Example 49

Agogic accent

An *agogic accent* (Gk. *agogos*, leading or drawing forth) results from a longer duration of a note.

Example 50

A combination of these accents, in very obvious form, is illustrated in Example 51:

Example 51

Syncopation

Syncopation is the term which denotes the interruption of normal (i.e., expected) rhythm, accent, or meter. Its use, or equivalency, is first found in the music of the French *Ars Nova* in the fourteenth century and has been observed in all Western music since that time.

A common change in rhythm is shown in Example 52:

Example 52

Similarly, a change in accent is "unexpected" (Example 53):

Example 53

Example 53 illustrates an actual duple meter within the confines of a ternary meter. (Compare to Example 54.)

Example 54

A change of meter is another possibility of disturbing the normal pulse (Example 55):

Example 55

Hemiola

Hemiola (Gk. *hemi–*, half), when referring to time values, denotes the relationship of 3:2. It is the play of twice three units against thrice two units, either simultaneously or successively. Two common successive examples are shown in Example 56:

Example 56

a.

b.

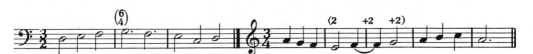

The term is also used, less accurately, to describe a vertical (simultaneous) combination of three against two (Example 57):[1]

Example 57

Polyrhythm

Polyrhythm denotes the simultaneous use of two or more different (and contrasting) rhythmic schemes (Example 58). Polyrhythms were prominent in the music of the fourteenth and early fifteenth centuries and again are a striking feature of twentieth-century rhythmic organization.

---

[1] The preferred term for a vertical two against three (Example 57) is *sesquialtera*.

Example 58

Polymetric

The term *polymetric* should be used to describe compositions which are notated in more than one meter simultaneously (Example 59):

Example 59

Isorhythm

Isorhythm is a term used to describe a constructive device frequently observed in fourteenth-century motets. Briefly, isorhythm provides for a consistent (or frequent) reiteration of a rhythmic pattern, as in Example 60:

Example 60*

*The bracketed pattern in this example is called a talea.

"Motor" rhythm

A recently coined term which describes constant motion in one or several parts is *motor rhythm* (Example 61):

Example 61

RHYTHMIC
CONTROLS

The control of rhythm on the part of the composer is as challenging as the control of other elements—melody, harmony, texture, and color. After establishing a rate or tempo, the rhythmic requirements should include both *predictability* and *surprise*. Observe the following examples:

Example 62

Fast:

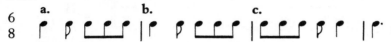

a. Neutral
b. Neutral or predictable
c. Surprise

Moderately slow:

a. Neutral
b. Surprise
c. Predictable
d. Surprise

Fast:

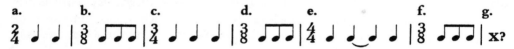

a. Neutral
b. Surprise
c. Predictable; the extra beat is surprise
d. Predictable
e. 4/4 is predictable; the tie is surprise
f. Predictable
g. X has, or should have, real suspense. Will the measure be 2/4, 3/4, 5/4, 3/8 or entirely different?

**Acceleration
and repose**

The rhythmic gesture may include a notated acceleration (*accelerando*):

Example 63

or a notated retard (*ritardando*):

Example 64

**Vital
and static**

If the rhythm is essentially unpredictable, or is marked by syncopations and accents, the effect is one of vitality (Example 65):

Example 65

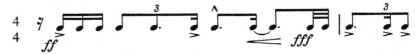

Conversely, an intentionally static composition, or section thereof, may be achieved by even and quite predictable rhythms (Example 66):

Example 66

**Thrust
and stability**

Obviously, a rhythmic pattern may begin on a strong beat, a weak beat, or with an *upbeat*. Each of these will have a pronounced effect on the expressive quality of the music (Example 67):

Example 67

provides for stability—appropriate for a March

provides for thrust, direction, or movement towards a specific point of repose (cadence)

has a similar effect of achieving thrust by the use of an upbeat, called *anacrusis*. The initial value of the anacrusis is subtracted from the final measure.

Rubato

Rubato, a performance practice appropriate for certain periods and styles, is the antithesis of rhythmic precision. The term is used to describe the gradual quickening or slowing down within a phrase or section. A typical *rubato* might approximate the re-notated version shown in Example 68:

Example 68

*The apostrophe (') is called an *atem* and is used by vocalists and instrumentalists as a breathing point in lieu of a notated rest.

Metronome

Rhythmic studies may be assisted by the use of the *metronome*, an instrument which measures the rate of motion per minute. Invented by Maelzel in the early nineteenth century, the apparatus is commonly used by composers to indicate a specific tempo. M.M. ♩ = 120 stands for Maelzel Metronome, with a setting of 120 oscillations per minute, with the quarter note used as the unit of measure.

A composition in 4/4 meter (♩=120) will require 30 measures for one minute of music:

$$\frac{4 \times X}{120} \qquad 4X = 120 \qquad X = 30$$

Similarly, 30 measures in 3/8 meter at ♪= 90 will have a duration of one minute:

$$\frac{3 \times 30}{90} = 1 \text{ (minute)}$$

**SUGGESTED
STUDIES**

1. Learn the rhythmic terminology in current use.
2. Study and practice conducting patterns.
3. Sing and study musical examples which contain varied accents, syncopations, hemiola, isorhythm, or polyrhythms.
4. Invent a short rhythmic composition (without pitches) which illustrates predictability and surprise, acceleration and repose, thrust and stability.

7

MELODY
CONTOUR
MELODIC CONSTRUCTION
MELODIC COMBINATION

MELODY

Successive notes of varying pitch and duration produce *melody*. Western melody—including Gregorian chant, folk songs, and composed melodies in all media—evidences certain common principles of motion. (These common principles will be discussed later, pp. 43–44.)

CONTOUR

Melodic *contour* refers to shape and to the physical placement of pitches. By superimposing graphic or geometric designs over a staff, without the benefit of pitches and duration, one can create a basic outline which clearly illustrates the concept of melodic contour. Experimentations such as those in Example 69, including a subsequent filling-in of pitches, may not produce memorable and profound melody; yet the idea of contour and of the *visual* appearance of melody will have been realized.

Example 69

The number of possible melodic contours is infinite, since shape is the essence of creative imagination. The five examples which follow (70a–e) illustrate shape, contour, and gesture:

Example 70

a. Sequence: *Dies irae*

b. Excerpt: *The Silver Swan*, Orlando Gibbons (1583–1625). Observe the solution of balance, symmetry, and proportion in these 7 measures by Gibbons.

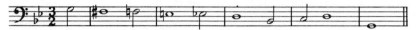

c. Ground bass: *Dido and Aeneas*, Henry Purcell (c. 1659–1695)

d. Excerpt: *Prelude to the Afternoon of a Faun*, Claude Debussy (1862–1918).

e. Excerpt: *String Quartet*, Op. 3 No. 5, Franz Joseph Haydn (1732–1809)

Dramatic shape

Example 70e illustrates one of the most common melodic shapes in Western music, a series of gradually rising pitches which reach a primary high point at approximately two-thirds or three-quarters of the total time-span. This contour, as well as any of the others quoted or observed, may also be applied to a composition as a whole. In that case the resultant contour is often referred to as the *dramatic shape* of music. Not infrequently, particular contours and dramatic shapes become part of a composer's identity. As an example, several of the melodies of Richard Strauss might be graphically shown as follows (Example 71):

Example 71

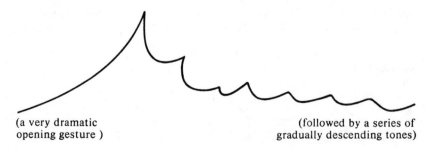

(a very dramatic   (followed by a series of
opening gesture)   gradually descending tones)

Similarly, Ernst Toch diagrammed the whole of the *"Meistersinger"*
Prelude of Richard Wagner (1813-1883) in the following fashion
(Example 72):

Example 72

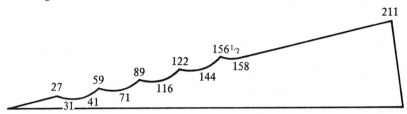

From Ernst Toch, *Shaping Forces in Music*, © 1948 Criterion Music Corp. Used by permission.

Melodic contour, as established by conjunct and disjunct motion,
ascending and descending motion, "gravity" or "pitch coils," thrust
and momentum, high-low turning points, is infinite in its variety,
behavior, and ability to fascinate.

Conjunct and disjunct motion   Melody of all periods and by all composers shows an interchange
between *conjunct* (step-wise) and *disjunct* (by leap) motion. Example 73
illustrates:

Example 73

a. Gregorian plainsong

Ky - ri - e   e   le - i - son   (iij)

b. Fifteenth-century folk song

L'homme, l'homme, l'homme ar - mé, l'homme ar-mé, L'homme ar-mé doibt on   dou - ter.

c. Eighteenth-century symphonic theme, Franz Joseph Haydn

d. Nineteenth-century operatic *motiv*, Richard Wagner

e. Turn-of-the-century, symphonic "harmonic-group," Claude
Debussy

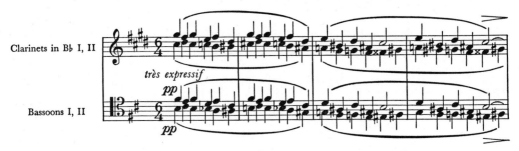

Clarinets in B♭ I, II

très expressif

pp

Bassoons I, II

pp

f. Twentieth-century orchestral subject, Béla Bartók

Andante tranquillo (♩ =ca 116-112)

pp con sord.

Compare these examples with two invented fragments which do
not balance conjunct and disjunct motion. In Example 74 the pitches
become predictable *in kind*. (Psychologically, one stops listening after
a short period of time.) Similarly, the constant disjunct motion of
Example 75, while not exactly boring, does lack balance. Obviously
there are occasions when a composer deliberately utilizes these types
of consistent motion for reasons of predictability and variety within
the total fabric of a composition.

Example 74

Andante

p

Example 75

Allegro

f

**Ascending and
descending motion**

It is apparent that melody is also a balance of *ascending* and *descending*
motion, as the previous examples illustrate. The movement in either
direction can comprise short gestures, as in the Wagner example, or
encompass a broad range (Example 76):

Example 76

Tone-row, *Violin Concerto* (1935), Alban Berg

Gravity

Melodic motion, in its physical behaviour, may be compared to *gravity*, in that opposing directions seek accommodation. Observe the two "gravitational pulls" in Example 77:

Example 77

Ricercar, *Dopo il Credo*, Girolamo Frescobaldi (1583-1643)

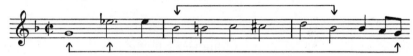

(The above example might be compared to two objects thrown into the air: the one that achieves the greater distance—g^i eb^{ii} g^i—takes longer to descend than the one traveling a shorter distance—bb^i d^{ii} bb^i.)

Pitch coils

Countless physical analogies can be made to pitch gestures. One additional comparison (Example 78) will suffice for illustration:

Example 78

Immer leiser wird mein Schlummer, Johannes Brahms

The behavior is that of a *coil*, which gathers tension when compressed and springs back to its natural shape when released. Musically, tension occurs from X to Y; release is established at Z.

Thrust and momentum

Thrust and momentum are difficult achievements without the dual components of pitch and duration sharing equally in tension and release.

Example 79

Fragment, *Fuga VIII*, *WTC* Vol. I, J. S. Bach

In Example 79, thrust is effected at *a,b,c,d,* and *e* for a variety of reasons:

Disjunct motion followed by conjunct motion

Changes in direction

Tied rhythm

Increase in motion, accomplished by the introduction of smaller note values

The point of greatest tension in measures 1–3 is at 79a; secondary tension is at 79b. Initial and interceding beats are either neutral or have varying degrees of relaxation.

**MELODIC
CONSTRUCTION**

The simplest, yet most profound, question one can ask when analyzing music is: How does the composer get from the first note to the last? (The fiction of literature and cinema offer strange answers!) The Bach fragment in Example 79 suggests several principles of *melodic construction.*

Control of high-low points

Control of contour (shape)

Control of tension and release

Implication of two voices from a single series

**Analysis of
Bach fragment**

Example 80

Observations:

1. 1–13 constitute the pitch series for the *subject* of the *D-sharp Minor Fugue.*
2. 3 is the primary high point (PHP).
3. 8 and 10 are secondary high points (SHP). (Observe that these SHP's are not repeated consecutively.)
4. 1 and 9 provide a tonic "anchor"; they are also primary low points (PLP).
5. 6 is a secondary low point (SLP); it is not repeated as a turning point.

Further observations:

1. Note the placement of 3, 8, 10 in time, which might be referred to as the "pacing of musical events."
2. Observe the spacing of relaxation (e.g., 4–7, 9, 11–13), which is nearly symmetrical after the first three pitches.
3. Note the placement of the secondary turning point (F♯ at 6), which occurs as the halfway point in terms of pitch, yet occurs at

the beginning of measure 2 in terms of rhythmic organization. This conflict of placement is one of the many features which yield the physical and psychological bases of music.

The contour of the Bach fragment may be shown graphically as:

Example 81

Observe also that the high and low turning points begin to suggest that two ideas, or forces, are present in a single line:

Example 82

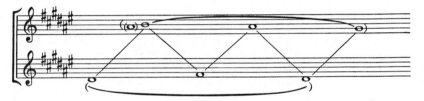

The basic musical gesture is probably the mainspring of composition. From this physical and psychological foundation, cells, motives, figures, subjects, themes, etc., can be fashioned in accordance with purely musical and expressive dictates.

Cell, figure, motive

The terms *cell*, *figure*, and *motive* are seemingly used synonymously (and rather subjectively) to describe the smallest unit of musical measurement. Of the three, the *motive* appears to have the sharpest identity and the greatest tenacity within a musical framework. The length of a motive varies from two to eight or nine notes; typically, the pitches are related to an easily recognizable rhythmic pattern. One further characteristic might be that the motive is often a part of and contributes to a larger pitch series, such as a theme. The *figure*, without this latter quality, has a less sharp profile in general. *Cell* is a particularly useful term for describing the two- or three-note groupings, recognizable but elusive, which permeate so much of the music of the Middle Ages and the twentieth century.

Subject, theme

The term *subject*—used in the seventeenth and eighteenth centuries for all kinds of ideas—most typically refers to a short pitch series related to a contrapuntal composition such as invention, ricercar, or fugue. *Theme* is used to describe a longer pitch series, most often in connection with a homophonic movement such as sonata, rondo, or variations.

Phrase, period

A *phrase* is an incomplete musical idea consisting of 6 to 8 notes in some examples of plainsong or chorales, or of 3 to 8 measures in traditional music. The *period* comprises 2 (or more) phrases, effecting a complete musical syntax. Much familiar music of the late eighteenth and nineteenth centuries, as well as an abundance of folk and popular music, contains a very orderly phrase-period organization:

Example 83

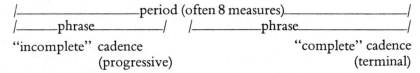

/————————————period (often 8 measures)———————————/
/———phrase————/   /———————phrase————————/
"incomplete" cadence   "complete" cadence
          (progressive)   (terminal)

**Subjective
description**

Subjective descriptions of melody—as static, quiet, lively, or dramatic —are derived from the combination of several factors:
    Tempo and dynamics
    Conjunct or disjunct motion
    Small or extended range
    Even or jagged rhythms
    Consistency or diverseness of ideas
Compare two obvious examples:

Example 84

a.

Andante

b.

Vivace

In current usage, the terms *polyphonic* and *contrapuntal* are synonymous in meaning and denote the combination of two or more independent melodic lines. The term *counterpoint* (L. *punctus contra punctum*, point against point) may be accurately interpreted as melody against melody.

**MELODIC
COMBINATION**

Even in the most linearly-conceived compositions, the vertical aspects must be considered. Both sixteenth- and eighteenth-century polyphony remain within the confines of an understandable harmonic framework. Polyphony varies from homophony in regard to rhythmic independence, interest between parts, and in achieving a meaningful melodic contour in each part.

Types of motion   Four types of melodic motion are associated with contrapuntal writing:

1. *Parallel:* in which the voices remain equidistant
2. *Similar:* in which the voices move in the same direction but change distance
3. *Oblique:* in which one voice remains stationary while the other(s) move
4. *Contrary:* in which the voices move in opposite directions

Example 85 illustrates:

Example 85

a. Parallel   **b.** Similar

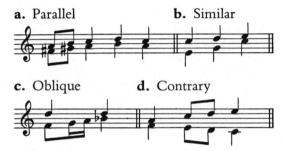

c. Oblique   **d.** Contrary

Observe the special employment of contrary motion in Example 86, which is a piano reduction of the opening measures of Arthur Honegger's *Symphony No. 5*.

Example 86

Excerpt, *Symphony No. 5*, Arthur Honegger (1892–1955)

Printed with authorization of Editions Salabert SA France, Copyright Editions Salabert, 1950. Piano reduction by Peter Hansen, *An Introduction to Twentieth Century Music*, Second Edition. © Copyright 1967 by Allyn and Bacon, Inc., Boston. Reprinted by permission of Allyn and Bacon, Inc.

**Contrapuntal
devices**

Contrapuntal devices refer to specific manipulations of pitches and their durations. A given melody, often called *cantus firmus* (L., fixed melody; pl. *cantus firmi*), is capable of appearing in several common forms:

Example 87

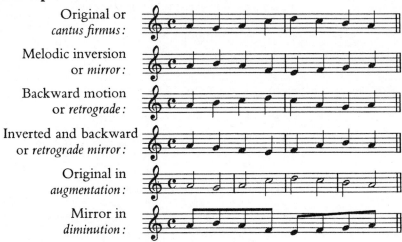

Original or
cantus firmus:

Melodic inversion
or *mirror:*

Backward motion
or *retrograde:*

Inverted and backward
or *retrograde mirror:*

Original in
augmentation:

Mirror in
diminution:

All of these devices have been known and used by composers from at least the fourteenth century onward.

**Imitation, canon,
Stimmtausch**

Imitation and *canon* (Gk., law, rule), as well as many of the so-called contrapuntal forms, are all *procedures* which adhere to certain principles of organization, in varying degrees of strictness.[1]

Imitation probably dates from Perotinus (c. 1225) and provides for a reiteration of a melodic idea in a different voice. The repetition is usually accomplished in one of three ways: in exact form—as the original (Example 88a); at a different pitch level—precise interval transposition from original (Example 88b); at a different pitch level—modified interval transposition from original (Example 88c):

Example 88

a. In exact form

---

[1] A canon in the Renaissance was any piece in which two (or more) people read differently from the same notation. The two voices often began together, but used different proportion signs and/or different clefs. For accurate performance, a directive was required. The directive was called *canon*.

b. Precise: at the major third above

c. Modified: at the sixth above (M6, M6, M6, m6)

The leading voice is called *dux*, while the voice making the repetition
is called *comes*. Voice exchange between two parts without interval or
octave modification is called *Stimmtausch*.

Imitation may be made of a few notes or of many. An entire composition in imitation is called a *canon*; early names for this procedure
include *rota*, *rondellus*, or *round*, of which *Sumer is icumen in*, dating
from about 1300, is an example:

Example 89

Excerpt, *Sumer is icumen in*

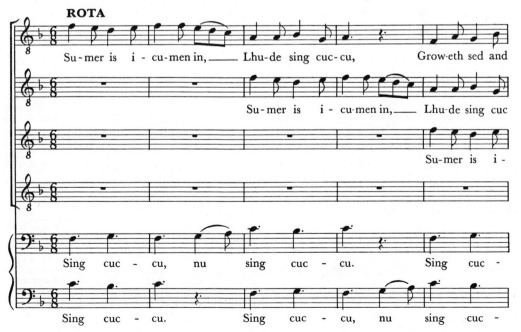

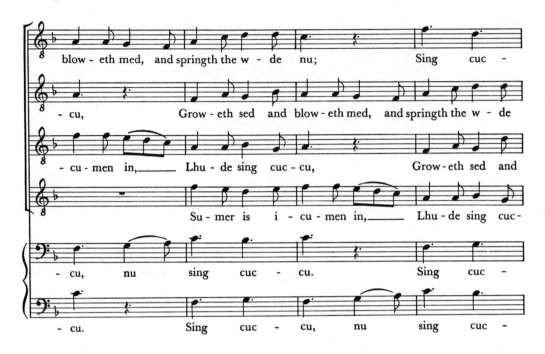

blow - eth med, and springth the w - de nu; Sing cuc -

- cu, Grow - eth sed and blow - eth med, and springth the w - de

- cu - men in,_____ Lhu - de sing cuc - cu, Grow - eth sed and

Su - mer is i - cu - men in,_____ Lhu - de sing cuc -

- cu, nu sing cuc - cu. Sing cuc -

- cu. Sing cuc - cu, nu sing cuc -

Canons are described according to the time interval, the pitch interval, and the contrapuntal device (if any) employed by the reiterating voice. The brief fragment, Example 90, may be identified as a canon

at two measures (time)
of the minor third above (pitch)
in retrograde inversion (devices)

Example 90

The canon has an intriguing history, spanning more than six hundred years. The student is referred particularly to the riddle canons of the fifteenth century, to the mensural canons of the fifteenth and sixteenth centuries, to the *Art of the Fugue* of Bach, and to the works of Webern and Dallapiccola for further investigations.

Ricercar, fugue, invention

Ricercar (It. *ricercare*, to seek out), *fugue* (L. *fuga*, flight), and *invention* (L. *inventione*) are polyphonic compositions employing imitative counterpoint. There is no set "form" for any of these compositions, although a few general observations regarding procedure can be made.

Imitative ricercar

1. As the instrumental counterpart to the sixteenth-century vocal motet, the ricercar usually has four or five independent voices.
2. Often, but not always, the ricercar is polythematic.
3. The ricercar is generally considered to have been the predecessor of the seventeenth- and eighteenth-century fugue.
4. Some examples are to be found in the twentieth century, among them, two in Stravinsky's *Cantata* (1951).

Fugue

1. Each fugue is written in a set number of voices; two-voice to five-voice are commonly found, with three or four parts being the norm.
2. Each voice is independent and participates in presenting the principal melodic material (subject).
3. The repetition of the subject, usually at the fifth above or the fourth below, is called an *answer*.
4. In the highly developed fugues of the eighteenth century, there is usually a *minimum* tonal scheme of at least three parts (e.g., tonic-dominant-tonic).
5. There are numerous fugues to be found in twentieth-century music literature; *Ludus Tonalis* by Paul Hindemith contains excellent examples.

Invention

1. Bach used the title "Inventiones" for fifteen two-part contrapuntal studies.
2. In this collection, each voice is of equal importance and participates in presenting, developing, and summarizing the musical ideas.
3. Some of the Bach *Inventions* illustrate specific constructive techniques, such as:
   a. motivic development: C major, e minor
   b. strict canon and invertible counterpoint (exchange of voices): c minor
   c. mirrors: E major
4. Imitation is usually at the octave, rather than at the fifth.
5. Several twentieth-century composers have written sets of inventions; the scenes of Act III of Alban Berg's opera *Wozzeck* are entitled "Inventions."

SUGGESTED
STUDIES

1. Examine melodies from diverse eras for observation of conjunct-disjunct balance; for constructive techniques of cell, figure, and motive; and for the graphic and dramatic shapes they present.

2. Examine melodies which utilize the devices of inversion, retrograde, and diminution.

3. Subject a melody of your choice to the devices of inversion, retrograde, and augmentation.

4. Write an original short canon; musical style should not be a consideration.

5. Analyze Bach's *Inventio 1* (Example 91) for melodic contours, treatment of subject, derivation of other musical ideas, and the overall design of the piece.

Example 91

Inventio 1, J. S. Bach (1685–1750)

8
COUNTERPOINT

The uniqueness of Western music lies in its fusion of horizontal (polyphonic) and vertical (homophonic) principles. Certain eras have become designated as polyphonic periods—specifically, the sixteenth, eighteenth, and twentieth centuries. As a result, there is a considerable neglect (which often prompts serious misunderstandings) of the music of the fifteenth, seventeenth, and nineteenth centuries as areas for contrapuntal studies.

COUNTERPOINT One can scarcely overestimate the value of the detailed study of counterpoint. In recent years, the eminent composers Roger Sessions and Luigi Dallapiccola both reaffirmed that the basic training of composers should be steeped in rigorous contrapuntal studies. Without question, profound insights, for all aspiring musicians, stem from a thorough knowledge of counterpoint.

The study of counterpoint is usually made on the basis of interval specification—i.e., of determining which intervals are appropriate for combination with an invented line or with a given melody (*cantus firmus*). In the sixteenth century, treatises dealt methodically with combinations, imitation, various types of counterpoint, and with canon; Zarlino's *Institutioni harmoniche* (1558), for instance, provided detailed explanations of these forms.

Examples 92–95, drawn from the fifteenth century to the twentieth century, illustrate various principles of control:
Control of melodic contours
Control of rhythmic thrust
Control of the interval distance between voices
Control of consonance and dissonance

Example 92

Excerpt, *Missa Sancti Jacobi*, Guillaume Dufay, fifteenth century

Example 93

Excerpt, *Missa: Prolationum*, Johannes Ockeghem, fifteenth century

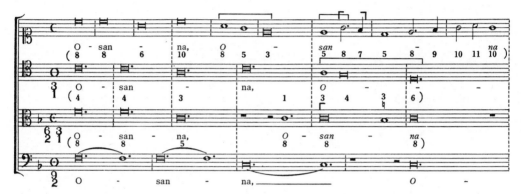

Example 94

Excerpt, *Chorale Prelude*, Samuel Scheidt, seventeenth century

Example 95

Excerpt, *Chromatic Invention*, Béla Bartók, twentieth century

**Species
counterpoint**

Current systematic study of contrapuntal techniques often begins with an investigation of *species counterpoint*. Here Johann Fux must be acknowledged for his treatise *Gradus ad Parnassum* (1725), which recommends an orderly course of study.

There are many reinterpretations of Fux—ranging from the rigorously disciplined to the nearly casual. The procedure set forth in Fux's treatise is appropriate for either the sixteenth-century or the eighteenth-century style. In the discussion of species counterpoint which follows, which is at once cursory and to a certain extent unorthodox, the examples are drawn from a single movement of a Bach *Suite* (see Example 101).

Example 96 (first species)

Extracted from J. S. Bach

Counterpoint:

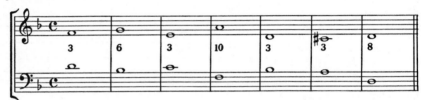

Cantus firmus:

Observations:

1. First species consists of a motion of one note of counterpoint for each note of *cantus firmus*.
2. Each line has a specific and independent contour.
3. Contrary motion is predominant.
4. Maximum sonority is achieved by the use of the intervals of thirds and sixths.

NOTE: Perfect consonants and dissonants are, of course, also acceptable. Octaves and fifths are sparingly used in two-voice texture because of the "thinness" of sound; the dissonance of seconds, sevenths, and tritones should be resolved—preferably by the use of contrary or oblique motion.

Example 97 (second species)

Extracted from J. S. Bach

Counterpoint:

Cantus firmus:

Observations:

1. Second species consists of two notes of counterpoint for each note of *cantus firmus*.
2. Each line is independent and contoured.
3. Imperfect consonants predominate; ninths and sevenths are resolved; the tritone is approached and quitted in contrary motion; perfect fifths are followed by sixths.

NOTE: In Fux, the first note on a downbeat (two half notes to a whole note) was invariably a consonance.

Example 98 (third species)

Extracted from J. S. Bach

Cantus firmus:

Counterpoint:

Observations:

1. Third species consists of three or more notes (4,6,8,9, etc.) of counterpoint to one note of *cantus firmus* (in Fux, third species meant four to one).
2. All intervals are employed; dissonants are resolved.
3. Contrary motion to the *cantus firmus* occurs typically on the first beats.

Example 99 (fourth species)

Extracted from J. S. Bach

a.   b. Inverted Cpt.

Cantus firmus:

Counterpoint:

Observations:

1. Fourth species consists of two notes of counterpoint for each note of *cantus firmus* and further includes the use of tied notes and a particular device called *suspension*. In each instance (in Fux, called *ligature* or *syncopation*), a consonant is tied over the bar, creating a

dissonant (second or seventh), which then is resolved on the weak
beat to a consonant third or sixth. An explanation of suspension is
found on p. 103.

2. Tied notes and suspensions may alternate with "free" counterpoint.

Example 100 (fifth species)

Extracted from J. S. Bach.

Observations:

1. In fifth species, a free number of notes are invented for each note
of *cantus firmus* or, as in the above example, the *cantus* and counterpoint are coequals.
2. Control of line, dissonance, and rhythmic interest is maintained.

One of the most engaging movements of Baroque keyboard
literature is the Minuet II from the *French Suite in D Minor* of Bach
(Example 101). The subtle changes in rhythm, texture, register, and
tonality enhance the symmetrical proportion. The middle voice, with
the exception of measures 5 and 6, has a sustaining or "pedal" role; the
outside voices are essentially curvilinear—balancing conjunct-
disjunct motion, tension and repose.

Example 101

Excerpt, *French Suite No. 1*, J. S. Bach (1685–1750)

Minuet II

The contrapuntal ideal is an interwoven web of sonority, propelled by rhythmic thrust, and controlled by harmony, texture, and color. No composition is completely lacking in contrapuntal implication— be it a single-line melody or a series of block chords. The strength and quality of the counterpoint, real or implied, is often a decisive factor in determining the aesthetic value of a composition.

SUGGESTED
STUDIES

1. Examine two-voice examples for observation of the composer's control of motion and dissonance.

2. Write an example of each species, above or below the given *cantus firmus*. (The original form may be found in Bach's *Art of the Fugue*.)

NOTE: Although it is not expected that the student be proficient in writing counterpoint after this brief introduction, the shaping of a good line and the control of consonant and dissonant intervals are reasonable expectations.

9

TEXTURE

ACCOMPANIMENT

SPATIAL ORGANIZATION

TEXTURE

Texture is a term which is applied to a number of phenomena in music. The common descriptions of texture—monophonic, polyphonic, homophonic, and heterophonic—have already been cited.

Monophony and polyphony emphasize the horizontal dimension of music; homophony underscores the vertical dimension; heterophony is a combination of these two dimensions. A canon is sometimes referred to as a diagonal relationship which reinforces the two-dimensional texture.

Descriptive terminology is used to indicate the number of participating voices, such as *thick* (or heavy) and *thin* (or light). The two fragments below could be described in these subjective terms:

Example 102

a. Thick   **b.** Thin

ACCOMPANI-MENT

Texture plays a far more important role in music than is often understood. Accompaniments; the *Alberti bass* (see below) and its progeny; inner pedals; and harmonic oscillations are methods of providing a backdrop for a musical action which is in the foreground. Often, accompaniment is the element of texture that "glues a piece together," covers the composer's thematic and structural seams, and establishes a continuity of sound.

As early as in the Vivaldi *Concerti*, and again in the Classical period (for example, see Mozart's *Symphony No. 39 in E flat*), extended passages are essentially non-thematic. In these areas, texture and rhythm become *emphasized* elements.

Example 103 illustrates a middle-range texture which provides harmonic filler, an inner pedal (g^1), and rhythmic motion:

Example 103

Voice or instrument:

Motion and pedal:

Melodic bass:

Alberti bass

Named after Domenico Alberti (1710-1740?), the *Alberti bass* consists of broken-chord figurations and was useful as middle-range accompanimental texture. Although overused and maligned, the Alberti bass offered some rhythmic viability in an otherwise static harmonic situation (see Example 106).

Classical accompanimental configurations have been modified in the nineteenth and twentieth centuries to accommodate style. Their musical function, however, remains the same—to provide motion.

Example 104

Nineteenth-century solution, similar to those of Chopin or Rachmaninoff

Example 105

Twentieth-century solution, similar to those of Stravinsky or
Bartók

Seventeen measures, excerpted from Mozart's *Concerto for Piano and
Orchestra*, K. 595 (Example 106), illustrate the function and importance of texture.

Example 106

Excerpt, *Piano Concerto*, K. 595, Wolfgang Amadeus Mozart (1756–
1791)

Observations:

1. Superimposed on the piano solo are light woodwind textures which "breathe" (measures 2–7).
2. The woodwind background changes from detached to sustained (measures 2–7 versus 8–10).
3. The strings add a new color and dynamic (measure 10).
4. The strings of measure 10 *generate* the solo of measure 11.
5. The strings in measures 14–16 relate to the solo of measures 1–7.

Although music is usually referred to as being two-dimensional, a third dimension is both seen and heard, especially in orchestral music. Example 107 charts these dimensions:

Example 107

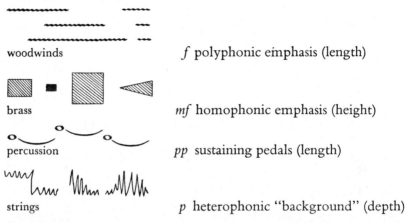

woodwinds   *f* polyphonic emphasis (length)

brass   *mf* homophonic emphasis (height)

percussion   *pp* sustaining pedals (length)

strings   *p* heterophonic "background" (depth)

These differing functions and dynamics provide for "layers of sound," not dissimilar to a third dimension. Gabrieli's polychoral works, the Berlioz and Benjamin Britten *Requiems*, Varèse's *Poème Électronique*, are all compositions which insist on a spatial organization of sound sources (i.e., wide separation of the different instrumental, vocal, or electronic "choirs"). Such arrangements tend to emphasize the dimension of depth.

Spatial organization may be realized by playing a different instrument, pitch, and dynamic from each corner of a classroom. Under such conditions, an ordinary e minor triad will suddenly have new life and potential.

Example 108

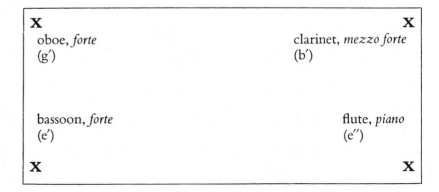

X	**X**
oboe, *forte* (g')	clarinet, *mezzo forte* (b')
bassoon, *forte* (e')	flute, *piano* (e'')
X	**X**

10

TIMBRE

COLOR

INSTRUMENTATION

TIMBRE

Timbre denotes the quality or "color" of a tone which, as previously stated, is determined by the relative intensity of the overtones.

COLOR

Color is a term most typically used to describe instrumental combinations. "Dark" and "bright" are in common usage and, although subjective, do have a physical basis, provided by a conflict (or lack thereof) of multiple overtone series. In *highly exaggerated* dynamics, two chords with their partials are illustrated (each sounding note is in itself a fundamental):

Example 109

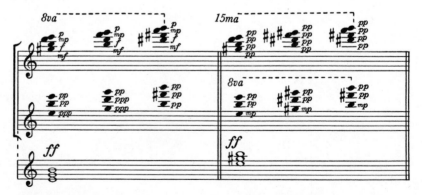

a. Three oboes:
   "dark"

b. Three flutes:
   "bright"

The fourth and fifth harmonics on the oboe are prominent, which accounts not only for its so-called nasal quality, but presents strong conflicts among the overtones when the three oboes are scored chordally (Example 109a). (Observe the "rub" of the G♯-G♮'s; of the D♮-D♯.) For the flutes, however (Example 109b), the most prominent overtone is the second partial, establishing a "clearer" basic tone and presenting fewer conflicts when used vertically. The higher octave is also a significant reason for the brighter sound.

**INSTRUMEN-
TATION**

**The orchestral
page**

Initial observations concerning an orchestral page include:

1. The order of instruments from top to bottom is: woodwinds; brasses; percussion; harp (also piano; solo, if any; voices, if any); and strings (Example 110).
2. In most instances, the instruments within each section are placed from high-sounding to low-sounding. The principal exception is that horns, which relate to both woodwinds and brass, are placed above trumpets on the page.
3. The tempo indication is placed above the woodwinds and often above the strings.
4. Dynamics are placed below the notes for instruments, and above the notes for voices.
5. The variety of key signatures is caused by the fact that some instruments are *transposing* instruments (i.e., sound at a different interval than written).

Transposition

Standard orchestral instruments which *transpose* are the English horn, clarinet, French horn, and trumpet. The piccolo sounds an octave higher than written, while the double bass and contrabassoon sound an octave lower. Transpositions are named according to the note that sounds when a written C is played. In all cases, it is a matter of exact compensation. For example, any instrument sounding a major second lower must be written a major second higher than the desired concert pitch. Common transpositions are illustrated in Example 111.

Key signatures often correspond to the transposition interval. Therefore, for a composition in C major, the signatures will correspond to those illustrated in Example 112.

Twentieth-century compositions without key signatures will typically have no signatures for the orchestral instruments, although the usual transpositions will be in effect.

In current practice, one also observes scores which are written at concert pitch. The composer usually mentions this fact on the title or instruction page. In such cases, transpositions must be made for the performers' parts (i.e., one does not expect the performer to transpose at sight or to write out the transposition.)

Example 110

Excerpt, *Symphony No. 8*, Ludwig van Beethoven

Symphonie No. 8

I

EXPOSITION

L. van Beethoven, Op. 93
1770—1827

Allegro vivace e con brio (♩. = 69)

Example 111

All *written* notes to sound c^i:

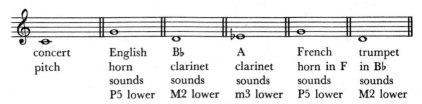

concert pitch	English horn sounds P5 lower	Bb clarinet sounds M2 lower	A clarinet sounds m3 lower	French horn in F sounds P5 lower	trumpet in Bb sounds M2 lower

The trumpet in F (Example 110) sounds a perfect fourth higher than written.

Example 112:

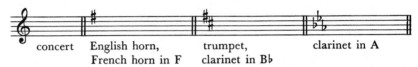

concert	English horn, French horn in F	trumpet, clarinet in Bb	clarinet in A

SUGGESTED STUDIES

1. Make a reduction of the Beethoven excerpt, Example 110, for piano, four-hands. Transpositions must be considered for the following instruments: clarinets, French horns, trumpets.
2. Transcribe about 16 measures of the vocal line of a Schubert (or similar) song for a clarinet in Bb.

11

INSTRUMENTS
INSTRUMENTAL
COMBINATION

INSTRUMENTS   A knowledge of instrumental ranges, transpositions, relative dynamic strength in each register, the individual sound in combination with other instruments, and special effects is essential for an enquiring musician. Possible and practical ranges, together with transpositions, are listed below.

Example 113

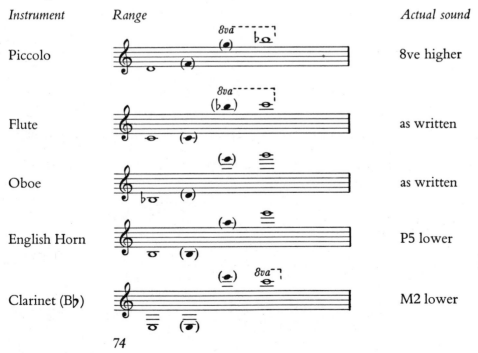

Instrument	Range	Actual sound
Piccolo		8ve higher
Flute		as written
Oboe		as written
English Horn		P5 lower
Clarinet (B♭)		M2 lower

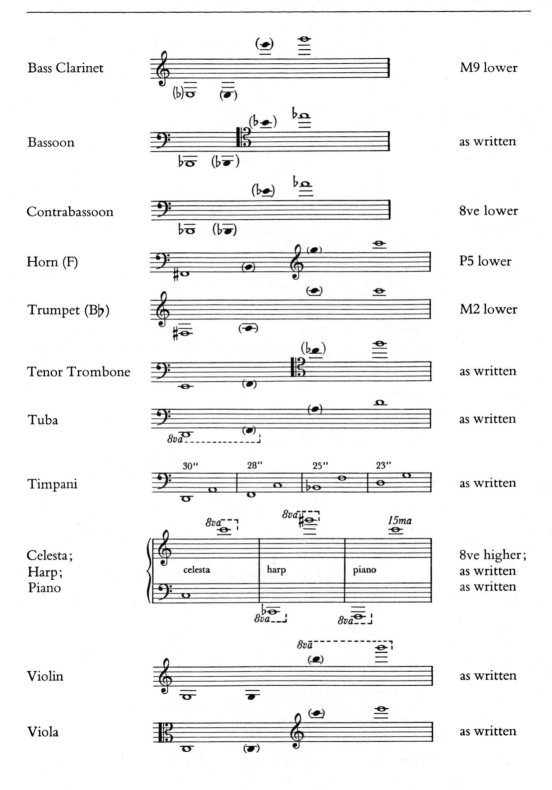

Cello

as written

Double Bass

8ve lower

NOTE: It is suggested that, if possible, each instrument be demonstrated in the classroom.

INSTRUMENTAL COMBINATION

In traditional scoring, several principles are observed, each of which requires considerable knowledge and experience before it is completely mastered and used with sophistication. These principles include: vertical balance, horizontal balance, textural balance, pedals, disposition in relationship and in opposition to the overtone series.

Vertical balance

Vertical balance is achieved by specific combination of instruments, agreement with the overtone series, dynamic adjustments, and placement in terms of range. Example 114 illustrates three possibilities—from an infinite number:

Example 114

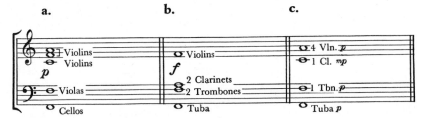

Observations:

1. Chord *a* is balanced in terms of tone color, strength of each instrument group, dynamics, and agreement with the overtone series.
2. Chord *b* is not balanced. Two clarinets in this range are not equal to the very prominent trombones; there is little homogeneity of sound; the clarinet note, a, is counter to the natural series.
3. Chord *c* retains some questionable features; a partial balance is obtained by dynamic adjustment. Chord *c* is not a typical combination in traditional (i.e., eighteenth- and nineteenth-century) scoring.

Generally speaking, in chordal progressions or in a contrapuntal texture of equal voices, an even vertical balance is desirable. Most orchestral music is, of course, beyond these limited categories. In a composite texture of melodic, accompanimental, and supporting bass functions, the vertical balance is appropriately adjusted by the composer.

Example 115

Melody :	strong
Accompaniment :	relatively weak
Bass :	weaker than melody, stronger than accompaniment

Horizontal balance

Horizontal balance in traditional scoring involves at least three different considerations:

1. Equal voicing in a contrapuntal texture.
2. Careful voice leading in general, including the resolution of dissonant intervals and the maintenance of a logical line, appropriate for the style.
3. The development of a musical logic in each part and for the instrumental design as a whole.

Textural balance

Textural balance provides for both contrast and unity. Passages employing the full orchestra (*tutti*) are typically contrasted by sections for fewer instruments or for specific colors.

The excerpt from *Romeo and Juliet* (Example 116) reveals several principles of traditional scoring.

Observations:

Measure 1. The string sonorities are balanced in terms of weight and dynamics.
The harp adds color—observe the dynamic specification.
A low pedal is provided by the bassoon.
Punctuation comes from the plucked double bass.
Measure 2. Flutes and oboes, staggered in their entries, provide motion.
Measure 3. The melodic line is high and bright and is capable of penetrating through the orchestral mass.
The remaining woodwinds effect an harmonic background.
A single horn carries a counter-motive—observe the high tessitura.
The violins and violas have a textural function—observe dynamic.
Cellos and double basses punctuate.
Measure 4. Observe the separation of the two oboes from a unison to octaves.

Example 116

Excerpt, *Romeo and Juliet*, Peter Ilich Tschaikovsky (1840–1893)

The twentieth century has elicited new attitudes from most composers regarding orchestral scoring. Example 117 illustrates a few techniques of more recent vintage: disposition in opposition to the overtone series, multiple pedals, *Klangfarben* (see p. 239) procedures, and improvisation:

Example 117

* Clarinet and horns are written at concert pitch.

SUGGESTED
STUDIES

1. Learn the range **and** transposition (if any) for each of the orchestral instruments which have been listed.

2. Arrange the following progression for large orchestra:

12

MUSICAL SYNTHESIS

FORM IN MUSIC

MUSICAL SYNTHESIS   *Synthesis* is the combination of separate substances, elements, or subordinate parts into a new construction or composition. The term might well be used, especially in initial studies, as a replacement for "form," which has variable meanings as well as implied limitations.

FORM IN MUSIC   A musical composition is the combination of pitches, durations, timbres, and, in most music, simultaneities of sound. Any such combination, placed in time, will create shape, design—or, in current musical parlance, *form*. In broadest terms, a composition is a sequence of musical events. Another definition, attributed to Pierre Boulez, is that of "a counterpoint of sound and silence." These definitions are, of course, entirely quantitative. Yet any group of sounds which "puncture" silence—no matter how seemingly disparate, illogical, or mutually incompatible—do produce shape. In short, nothing exists in time or space without *shape*.

One of the most succinct, yet meaningful and accurate definitions of "form" is that of Wallace Berry: "form is the sum of those qualities in a piece of music that bind together its parts and animate the whole."[1] In discussing musical form, the phrase "form *in* music" is often applied. This is a broad phrase possibly implying a predetermined *design* of some kind. Its use is preferable, however, to use of "forms *of* music", for in that phrase lies the persistent connotation of

---

[1] Wallace Berry, *Form in Music* (Englewood Cliffs, N.J.: Prentice-Hall, 1966), Preface, unnumbered.

a mold into which the composer pours the musical elements and a few performance instructions.

There is no one fugal *form* nor, indeed, one sonata *form* or rondo *form*; it is the very diversity of these procedures and general designs which, in part, renders them worthy of aural and intellectual consideration. Investigation of Western music from all periods seems to suggest, instead, *principles of organization* which apply, in varying degrees, to broad categories of musical design.

Organization requires control. From among the numerous factors of control considered by the composer, a few of the most essential are cited:

Control factors

1. Control of dynamic and static gestures
2. Control of repetition and variation principles
3. Control of internal arrival points
4. Control of phrasing and cadencing
5. Control of tonal orientations or implications
6. Control of texture and color
7. Control of the pacing of musical events, assisted by tempo and dynamics
8. Control of the relationships between the subparts and the whole (i.e., microform–macroform correlations)

Logic and coherence

No single set of axioms guarantees a satisfying design; yet these control factors can, in the best of circumstances, achieve the ultimate goals of musical design, which are *logic* and *coherence*.

The following five principles may assist in the understanding of musical organization:

1. *Principle of contrast:*
   (I, of musical ideas):

a	b	
a	b	a

   a   b   binary (bi-partite)
   a   b   a   ternary (tri-partite), aria

2. *Principle of contrast:*
   (II, of tonal schemes):

first tonal area	second tonal area	varied tonal areas	first tonal area	sonata (single movement)

3. *Principle of repetition:*

   a a a a etc., or   strophic
   ab ab ab ab etc.
   a b c a d a...   rondeau, ritornello
   A B A$^{(')}$C A$^{(')}$ small rondo
   A B A$^{(')}$C A$^{('')}$B$^{(')}$A$^{(''')}$ large rondo

4. *Principle of variation:*

    a. An idea subjected to a changing environment, or   *cantus firmus* mass
    ricercar
    fugue
    passacaglia
    chaconne

    b. A musical idea constantly modified   Baroque, Classic, Romantic variations

5. *Principle of contiguity:*

    A constantly evolving matrix of sound. The German term *durchkomponiert* (through-composed) has similar implications   through-composed songs
    most canons
    "continual" variations

It is immediately apparent that most compositions combine two or more of these organizing principles. Perhaps the greatest obstacle to a musical understanding of new or unfamiliar music is the elusiveness of the design or one's lack of comprehension of it. It is essential that one should learn, through listening and analyzing, to grasp the architectural and dramatic shapes of music and the relationship of the parts to the totality. Since no two pieces are identical, it is reasonable to suggest that each composition be accepted (or rejected) on, and in, its own terms.

SUGGESTED
STUDIES

1. It is suggested that readings be undertaken on the procedures and forms cited on the preceding pages. Possible sources: *Harvard Dictionary; Groves' Dictionary of Music and Musicians.*
2. Aural analysis, observing the principles of organization, is recommended.
3. Basic study of phrase and period structure, as well as of simple binary and ternary principles, should be made.

PART II

The Triadic Basis

"Everything is in flux."
— *Heraclitus*, c. 500 B.C.

13

HARMONIC EVOLUTION

SECULAR MONODY

DETERMINATION OF ROOTS

**HARMONIC
EVOLUTION**

Tertian harmony evolved over a span of several hundred years—its emergence, development, and supercession generally relating to the broad period 1450 to 1950.[1] The term *tertian* (L. *tertianus*, third) simply refers to the calculation and organization of pitches in series of thirds: C E G B D F A C.

Certainly numerous influences contrived to effect the orderly and sophisticated tertian system. Initial investigation should consider both sacred and secular musical composition; melody and harmony as separate, interrelated, and combined evolutions; and the countless X-factors of insatiable curiosity and experimentation on the part of musicians.

Examples 118 through 123 give a cursory view[2] of some of the processes which pointed toward a tertian system:

Example 118

Free Organum: *Cunctipotens genitor*, eleventh century

Example 119

Melismatic Organum: *Cunctipotens genitor*, c. 1125

---

[1] Willi Apel gives these dates as 1450-1900.
[2] Examples 118–123 are found in *Historical Anthology of Music,* Vol. 1, pp. 22, 23, 30, 40, 56, 66.

Example 120

Fragment, Clausulae, *Haec Dies*, in the style of Perotinus (?1160–1230)

Example 121

First part, rondeau type, *Dieu soit,* Adam de la Halle (c. 1230–1287)

Example 122

Fragment, Ballata: *Amor c'al tuo suggetto,* Francesco Landini (1325–1397)

Example 123

Motet, *Sancte Maria,* John Dunstable (c. 1370–1453)

These examples indicate a developing system of imperfect consonants as the principal sonority in music; the earlier practice of open fourths, fifths, and octaves gave way to thirds and sixths; parallel motion, as an ideal, was replaced by the concept of contrary and oblique motion. Polyphonic idioms, such as cadences, in all probability prompted the consideration of *harmony*, per se.

SECULAR
MONODY

Aside from its poignant beauty, the Minnesinger *May-Song* provides abundant insight into the art of *secular monody* in the early thirteenth century:

Example 124

Minnesinger *May-Song*, Neidhart von Reuental (c. 1180–1240)

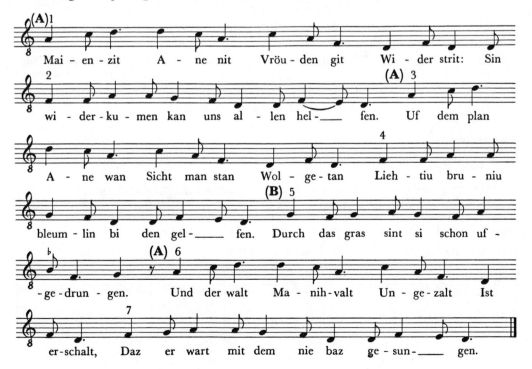

Transcribed by Edith Borroff. Used by permission.

Observations:

1. The composition suggests motivic construction; the rhythmic figure ♩ ♪ ♩. is a modal pattern and has fourteen appearances in the course of the song.
2. The phrases are defined by the text, by contrast and repetition, and by tonal orientations.
3. The first two lines of the *May-Song* form a *period*, comprised of two phrases.
4. The seven phrases effect a *closed form:*

   A (ab)   A (ab)   B (c)   A (ab)
   period   period   phrase (?)   period

   A fascinating feature of this design is the functioning of *phrase c* as a complete period (*B*).
5. Regular rhythmic groupings occur throughout (a compound duple meter is suggested).
6. The line is curvilinear with considerable disjunct motion.
7. The tonal orientation, within the octave $d^i a^i d^{ii}$—with the final d^i—is dorian in character; the sixth degree is nearly avoided; an emphasis on g^i occurs in phrase 5, suggesting an early equivalent to modulation.
8. Tertian orientation is clearly suggested—to the extent that the *May-Song* becomes a study in thirds; substructure notes of phrases 1 and 2 establish two triads:

   $a^i d^{ii} a^i f^i d^i$ $f^i a^i (g^i) d^i$

**DETER-
MINATION OF
ROOTS**

In tertian harmony chords are spelled in thirds; the *root* is the starting note and no note must be extraneous, although notes may be omitted. In the composite D E G B, the root is E and the total chord spells as: E G B D. Four examples further illustrate:

Example 125

a. A single line   **b.** Two voices

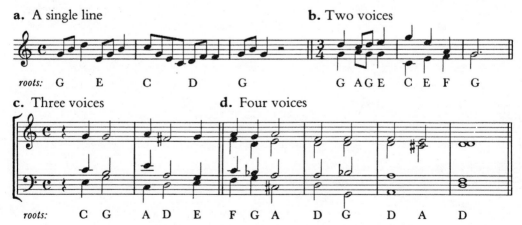

roots: G   E   C   D   G   G AG E   C E   F   G

c. Three voices   **d.** Four voices

roots: C G   A   D   E   F   G   A   D   G   D   A   D

Two observations are pertinent to the above examples:

1. Not all tones of a triad need be present for a clear determination of the root.
2. The root does not always appear in the bass; rather, it may be given to any voice.

Triad

The *triad*, a tertian sonority of three different pitches, is described by the bass note:

Bass note	Description	Name
root of chord	root position	chord of the fifth
third of chord	first inversion[1]	chord of the sixth
fifth of chord	second inversion	six-four chord

Root movement

Root movement is a term used to describe the scale distance between vertical sonorities:

Example 126

by seconds   by thirds   by fourths   by fifths

Often the style of a particular era or of an individual composer will reveal a marked preference for certain kinds of root movement. As a general observation, not to be interpreted too literally, composers in the Renaissance often favored root movement by seconds and thirds, except at cadence points where movement by fourths and fifths is predominant; the emphasized movement in the Baroque and Classical periods is that of fourths and fifths; while the relationship of thirds was an important feature of the early Romantic period. Since that time, all possibilities have been rather freely employed—determined by the selective processes of the composer.

Example 127 yields an indication of fifteenth-century practice.

Example 127

Excerpt, Agnus Dei, *Ave Regine Coelorum*, Guillaume Dufay (1400-1474)

[1] A systematic theory of chord inversion was discussed by Jean-Philippe Rameau in *Traité de l'Harmonie* (1722) and *Nouveau système de Musique theorique* (1726).

Observe that all sonorities contain a minimum of one root and one third, with the exceptions of measures 7 and 11. The notes which are circled should be omitted from discussion at this time.

SUGGESTED
STUDIES

1. In Example 127, study the melodic motion of each line.
   What polyphonic procedure is employed in measures 1–7?
   What are the tonal orientations?
   Analyze the cadence practice.

2. Sing and analyze the following *Trouvère Ballade*:

Example 128

Trouvère Ballade, Colin Muset, after 1234

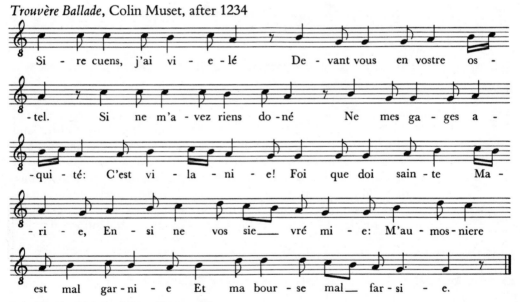

Si – re cuens, j'ai vi – e -lé   De - vant vous   en vostre   os -

- tel.   Si   ne m'a - vez riens   do -né   Ne   mes ga - ges   a -

-qui – té: C'est vi – la – ni – e!   Foi   que doi   sain - te   Ma -

– ri – e,   En – si   ne   vos   sie___   vré   mi – e: M'au - mos - niere

est   mal   gar - ni – e   Et   ma bour - se   mal__   far - si – e.

Transcribed by Edith Borroff. Used by permission.

Be able to discuss the following points:

a. The types of melodic construction: cells, motives, etc.
b. The internal organization: by phrases, periods, or other groupings
c. The overall design
d. The rhythmic groupings; the implied meters
e. The modal characteristics; the tonal orientation
f. Cadence practice

3. Create short compositions by completing the following fragments. Control the melodic contours so that they are complementary to that which is established:

Example 129

a. Dorian. Complete by adding 3 to 5 measures.

b. Phrygian. Complete by adding 4 to 6 measures.

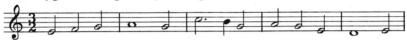

c. Mixolydian. Complete by adding 2 to 4 measures.

d. Aeolian. Two voices in thirds and sixths (8ᵛˢ at beginning and at cadences). Complete by adding 5 measures.

e. Ionian. Three-voice. Complete by adding one inner voice. The third of the chord must be present. Continue analysis with Roman numerals.

4. The *Praeambulum in re* (Example 130) is a short organ composition from the early sixteenth century. It is from the *tablature* of Leonhard Kleber *Historical Anthology of Music*, No. 84f).
Be prepared to discuss, or write a short analytical essay on, the following points:

   a. The complete meaning of the title; the meaning of *tablature* in this context
   b. The rhythmic aspects of the composition

c. The identification of mode and of tonal orientation
d. The contour of each line, with special attention paid to the outside voices
e. The root movement

Example 130

Praeambulum in re, Leonhard Kleber (c. 1490–1556)

14

FOUR-VOICE TEXTURE

STRUCTURE

DOUBLING

FOUR-VOICE TEXTURE

Early development of polyphony and harmony in Western music witnessed an extension in the number of parts used in a given composition: from monophonic to two-voice, typical in the eleventh and twelfth centuries; to three-voice, common from the thirteenth century on. Harmonic studies are usually centered around a four-voice texture. There are at least three explanations for this practice:

1. Music in four parts is abundant from the fifteenth century to the present.
2. Four parts offer equal representation of each voice type by range (soprano, alto, tenor, bass) from about 1550 onward.
3. Most of the mechanical problems which require investigation and technique in writing are in evidence in a four-voice texture.

Sixteenth- and seventeenth-century choral music was often written for five, six, or eight voices. Thomas Tallis' *Spem in alium nunquam habui*, an attempt at forty independent lines, is one of music literature's most exciting textures.

In the manipulation of four voices, one needs to keep in mind the connective processes in music. Although spelling, structuring, and doubling are crucial items of information, the triad has little significance without a context and an environment which provide for the connections of sound in time. There are two immediate problems, both of which require a comprehensive understanding. These are:

Four-voice structure (chord spacing)

Doubling (note repetition in a vertical sense)

STRUCTURE

In a homophonic four-voice texture there are two principal types of structure, commonly denoted as *open* and *close*.

95

Example 131

a. Open   **b.** Close

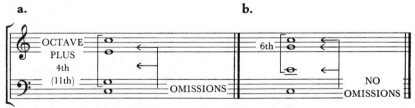

The *disposition* of the UPPER THREE VOICES determines the structure. Despite the musical importance of the bass, it is not a factor in structural disposition.

In open structure:

1. The distance between the soprano and tenor is *greater* than an octave.
2. The order, from the top down, is chord tone, omission, chord tone, omission, chord tone (Example 132a).

In close structure:

1. The distance between the soprano and tenor is *less* than an octave.
2. The upper three chord tones are immediately adjacent (Example 132b).

Example 132

a.   **b.**

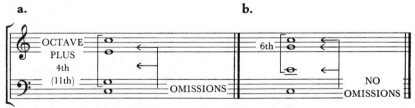

DOUBLING   Obviously, the utilization of a triad (three tones) in a four-voice setting necessitates the repetition or *doubling* of one of the notes. Despite disagreement among theorists, the student is advised to consider the following premise:

For major and minor triads in root position, DOUBLE THE ROOT.

Quite rightly, this premise is subject to modifications: for reasons of voice leading; when the root is an *altered* scale degree (this, in turn, may be modified depending upon context and function); or because of the preference of a composer for a particular kind of sonority and disposition—such as two roots, two thirds, and omission of the fifth.

The following are common exceptions to regular doubling:

1. Tripled root and one third—common in cadences of all periods (Example 133a)
2. One root, doubled third, one fifth—common in certain progressions, particularly V, VI in a minor key (Example 133b)
3. One root, one third, doubled fifth—for reasons of voice leading and when chords are repeated (Example 133c)

Example 133

a.   b.   c.

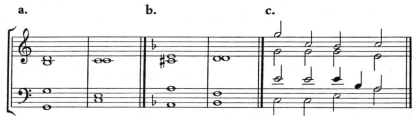

Example 134

From *Adoremus in Aeternum*, Gregorio Allegri (1560–1652)

Observations:

1. The root movement in Example 134 is that of a third, fourth, second, and fifth.
2. From 1 to 2 (third), the *common tones* are retained; the bass moves in *oblique* motion to the soprano.
3. From 2 to 3 (fourth), the common tone is retained and again *oblique* motion results between the outer voices.
4. From 3 to 4 (second), no common tones exist; therefore the bass and soprano move in *contrary* motion, while the inner voices move to the immediately adjacent chord tones.
5. From 4 to 5 (fifth), the bass moves *obliquely* to the held common tone in the soprano. The alto moves directly to the nearest chord tone c^i, while the tenor line contains a decoration and delay in its resolution to the half note a. The circled notes are discussed in Chapter 15.

Oblique and contrary motion effect a smooth, contiguous sound. For both aesthetic and mechanical reasons, contrary motion is often preferred. Oblique motion is common where roots are a third apart. Similar motion is frequently found where roots are a fourth or fifth apart, but here caution is necessary to avoid parallel perfect fifths and octaves.

Observations:

1. The entire example is in *close* structure.
2. The five major and minor sonorities each contain:
   Two roots
   One third
   One fifth

SUGGESTED
STUDIES

1. Analyze Example 135, to determine:

   a. The root movement of each progression together with the melodic movement of each voice
   b. The structure of each chord
   c. The doubling of each chord
   d. The chordal relationship to the tonic—I, V, etc.

Example 135

Ave Verum, Giacomo Carissimi (1604–1674)

2. Sing, play, and analyze the following invented examples (136–139), each of which illustrates a particular kind of root movement, melodic motion, and structure. The doubling is "regular" throughout.

Example 136

a.   b.

Example 137

Example 138

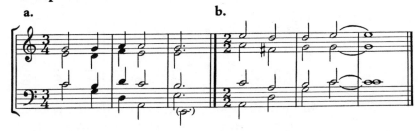

Example 139

3. For Example 140 (a–d), observe the following instructions:

    a. Use only major and minor sonorities in root position.

    b. All chords should preferably contain two roots, one third, one fifth.

    c. The structure should remain either open or close throughout.

Example 140

a. Adapted from *If ye love me*, Thomas Tallis (1515–1585). Complete in four parts by writing the alto and tenor voices. Use close structure.

b. From *Ave Verum*, Giacomo Carissimi (1604–1674). Add the three upper voices to the given bass line. Use open structure.

c. Invent an appropriate *consequent phrase* to the following *antecedent phrase*.

d. In the ionian mode (C major), 4/4 meter, invent a short composition—close structure, about 9 measures—which has the following progression.

I VI IV V III IV I V V VI II III IV I VI V I

4. The following study (Example 141) is adapted from a chanson of Orlandus Lassus (1532–1594).
   a. Complete the composition by adding two inner voices.
   b. Give a root-movement analysis of the composition.
   c. Be able to discuss the design and melodic contours.
   d. Compare with the original: *Bon jour, mon coeur.*
      What are the principal similarities?
      What are the principal differences?

Example 141

15

CHANGE OF STRUCTURE
NON-CHORD TONES
IRREGULAR DOUBLING
FIRST INVERSION
FAUXBOURDON
FIGURED BASS

CHANGE OF STRUCTURE Four different sonorities: tonic, dominant, subdominant, and submediant are utilized in Example 142. Within this restricted vocabulary, the composer balances repetition and variation and provides for a symmetrical period in essentially parallel construction. The fragment is the essence of harmonic simplicity.

Example 142

Excerpt, *Ave Maria*, attributed to Jacob Arcadelt (c. 1514–1575)

Bracketed chords in Example 142 show two common ways of accomplishing *change of structure* within the phrase:

1. Between repeated chords; any chord repetition permits the change of structure from close to open, or the reverse, open to close.
2. Between two chords whose roots are a fifth apart; typically, but not invariably, the third of one chord moves to the third of the next chord *in the same voice.* After the new structure has been established, normal doubling procedures apply.

NON-CHORD TONES

The circled notes (X, Y) in measure 7 of Example 142 are extraneous to the harmony, but of paramount significance to the musical fabric. Their function is that of melodic *connection* between two different chords—in this instance, from bb^i to f^i.

Passing tones

Typically these tones bridge a distance of a third or fourth; they are commonly called *passing tones.* The note marked X occurs on the weak part of the beat and is therefore *unaccented*; note Y appears on the strong part of the beat and is frequently denoted as *accented.* In this latter case (of an accented passing tone), a distinction is made by several writers who would refer to this note as an appoggiatura (It. *appoggiare*, to lean) (see p. 117). Of the several categories of non-chord tones—each with varied, and on occasion confusing, nomenclature—passing tones have been the most widely used by composers of all periods. Passing tones achieve a conjunct melodic motion between the essential chord tones of the basic sonorities.

Passing tones may function as connections in several different ways:

1. They may appear on a weak beat or a strong beat (Example 142).
2. They may ascend or descend in direction (Example 143a, b).
3. They may appear in more than one voice simultaneously (Example 143b, c).

Example 143

**Suspensions
(delayed non-chord
tones)**

A non-chord tone which is momentarily delayed in its normal movement or resolution is called a *suspension.*

The total suspension figure is comprised of:

1. *Preparation*: the note is prepared as an harmonic tone in the same voice. The rhythmic value of the preparation is usually equal to or greater than the suspension itself.

2. *Suspension*: the note becomes a dissonance on the accented part of the beat.

3. *Resolution*: the note resolves, usually step-wise down, on the unaccented part of the beat. Sometimes a distinction is made for the upward resolution of a suspension by calling it a *retardation*.

There are four common appearances of the suspension in parts above the bass: 2-1, 4-3, 7-6, and 9-8. The behavior of the 6-5 melodic figuration is closely related but contains no actual dissonance.

All suspensions in Example 146 are marked S. Additional illustrations are shown in Example 144.

Example 144

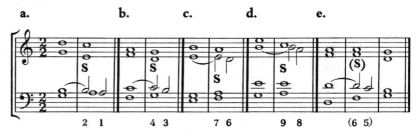

A majority of the above examples of suspension will be found in an ornamented and decorated version in the Palestrina composition, Example 151.

IRREGULAR DOUBLING

The asterisked (*) chords in Example 142 are instances of *irregular doubling*. In both cases they appear to be caused by the composer's desire to avoid parallel perfect fifths and octaves which would suddenly reduce four independent voices to one voice accompanied by three "shadows" (see Example 145).

The considerations of independence of line and consistency of texture seem to be logical explanations for the rather consistent avoidance of these parallel perfect consonants. Certainly there is no acoustical problem, nor are these parallels aesthetically unpleasant. Parallel perfect fourths are freely used in a texture of three or more voices, in all periods.

Example 145

a. Arcadelt   **b.** Invented with regular doubling

Josquin's eloquent 17 measures (Example 146) masterfully control both horizontal and vertical dimensions of sound.

Example 146

Excerpt, Agnus Dei, *Missa Pange Lingua*, Josquin des Prez (c. 1450–1521)

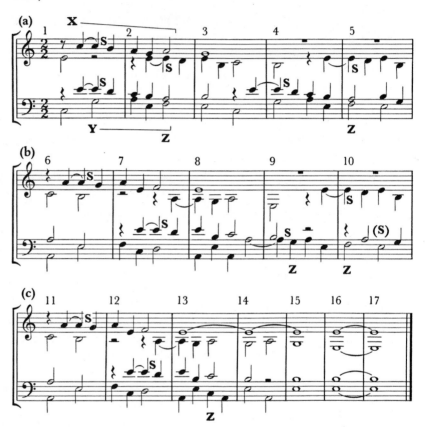

Observations:

1. The 17 measures suggest a grouping of three 5-measure phrases (*a, b, c*)—with the third phrase containing a 2-measure extension.
2. The organizing principles are those of contiguity and repetition.
3. Motivic construction is implied by the constant interplay, and imitative use, of two short musical ideas marked X and Y.
4. Root movement indicates a preference for seconds (12) and fifths (14), followed by fourths (8) and thirds (1).
5. The outside voices frequently complement each other with contrary motion; similar and oblique motion provide variety;

the occasional omission of the upper voice achieves subtle changes in texture and color.

All chords in Example 146 are in root position with the exception of those marked Z. These instances illustrate Josquin's use of the chord of the sixth.

<table>
<tr><td>

FIRST INVERSION
(Chord of the sixth)

</td><td>

A *chord of the sixth* (i.e., a chord in *first inversion*) is a triad in which the chord third is in the bass. Chords of the sixth have been freely utilized by all composers of the tertian period. In addition to their particular sonority, which enriches the harmonic resources of tertian music, sixth-chords have a pronounced effect on the contour of the bass line. By the simple alternation of root position and first inversion triads, the bass can become an entirely conjunct and contiguous line. Two observations are pertinent concerning the chord of the sixth:

</td></tr>
</table>

1. In a major or minor triad in first inversion, the soprano (upper voice) is often *doubled*.
2. Following a first inversion chord, a *change of structure* from open to close, or the reverse, may be made.

Common four-voice vocal dispositions are shown in Example 147:

Example 147

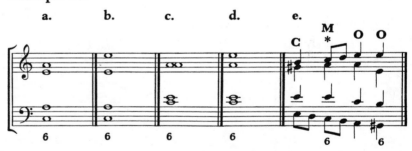

Example 147e illustrates a chord of the sixth (*) with the third in both the bass and soprano; this disposition is a convenient and effective use of the sonority as a passing chord. At this same point, the structure has changed from close to open; the measure itself is comprised of mixed structure (C M O O).

<table>
<tr><td>

FAUXBOURDON

</td><td>

The antecedents of first inversion chords include *fauxbourdon* and its counterpart, the *English discant*, which were procedures for improvisation with a *cantus firmus*. In Burgundian *fauxbourdon* the two outside voices were notated (the upper voice carrying the plainsong, transposed up an octave, and the lower voice moving in essentially

</td></tr>
</table>

parallel sixths below); the middle voice improvised a perfect fourth below the plainsong.

In English discant, the lowest voice was assigned the notated plainsong. The two upper voices then provided the sixth-chord motion according to set instructions and traditions.

Example 148

Excerpt, Worcester School, fourteenth century

(Blessed is the womb of the Virgin Mary.)

Quoted in *The New Oxford History of Music* (London: Oxford University Press, 1954), Vol. II, p. 351.

FIGURED BASS   *Figured bass*, or *through-bass*, is a system of musical shorthand which provides for a bass line and a set of numbers and symbols. The system evolved from the improvisational practices of the sixteenth century and was initially employed by Viadana, Croce, and others in the late sixteenth century; its use was nearly universal in the period 1600–1750. After 1750 figured bass was used for analysis and part-writing.

Example 149

Excerpt from continuo madrigal: *Amarilli mia bella*, Giulio Caccini (c. 1548–1618)

(Amarillis my beautiful, do you not believe, oh my heart's sweet desire, that you are my love.)

The numbers and symbols of the figured bass system indicate pitches to be sounded above the bass:

1. A triad in root position is usually without any figure—with the understanding in performance practice that the third and fifth above the bass are added as appropriate.
2. A triad in first inversion has the figures $\frac{6}{3}$ and is commonly abbreviated as 6.
3. An isolated accidental below the bass will always refer to the third (tenth, seventeenth) above the indicated note.
4. Any chromatic alteration must be shown; the placing of a sharp, natural, or flat immediately before the figure is the most common practice—although editorial procedures vary; the diagonal slash (/) or straight slash (—) through a figure indicates a sharping of that particular note.
5. Figures for compound intervals observed in Example 149, measure 9: 11 ♯10 14 were modified in a later period of history to their simpler forms: 4 ♯3 7. In all periods, however, the performer probably took certain liberties regarding the placement of the specific pitches; for example, g f♯ might also be g^i $f♯^i$.

Example 150 illustrates possible realizations of a given figured bass:

Example 150

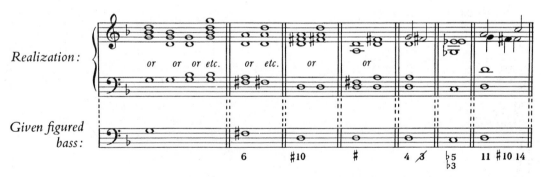

Realization:

or   or   or etc.   or   etc.   or   or

Given figured bass:

6   ♯10   ♯   4 ♂   ♭5   11 ♯10 14
                                                       ♭3

SUGGESTED
STUDIES

1. Analyze the following example in terms of:
   Root movement
   Melodic motion
   Structure of chords; changes in structure
   Doublings
   Non-harmonic tones: passing tones and suspensions
   Sixth chords

Example 151

O Bone Jesu (complete), attributed to Giovanni Pierluigi da Palestrina
(1524–1594)

2. Complete Example 152 to four voices, except where rests are
indicated. Include an harmonic analysis.

Example 152

Adapted from Christopher Tye (c. 1500–c. 1572)

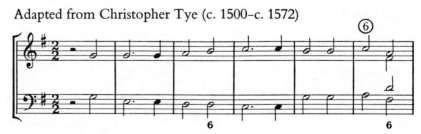

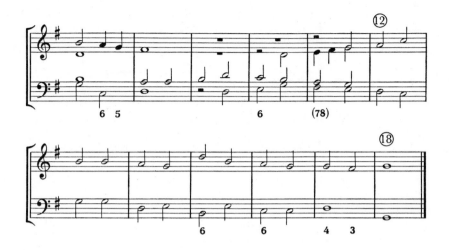

3. In Example 153, complete the figured bass to four parts. Use close structure and regular doublings. Include an harmonic analysis.

Example 153

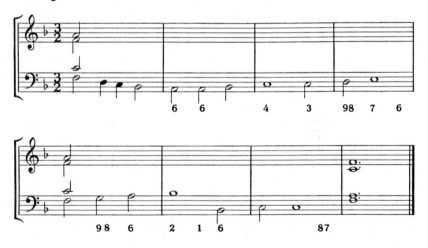

4. Complete Example 154 to four voices following the given Roman and Arabic numerals.

Example 154

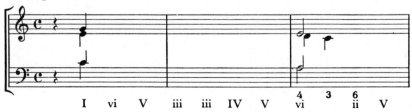

5. Invent two original phrases, using concepts illustrated in Suggested Studies 2, 3, and 4.

16

FUNCTIONAL HARMONY
DIMINISHED TRIADS
SECONDARY FUNCTION
EMBELLISHING TONES

FUNCTIONAL HARMONY

One of literature's most famous polyphonic songs is Heinrich Isaac's *Insbruck, ich muss dich lassen* (Example 155). In the quoted fragment, each line is independently contoured, yet the vertical situations are clearly defined. The example illustrates the use of the *diminished triad* and additional non-chord tones not previously discussed. At the same time, the Isaac song prompts a consideration of the ways in which harmonic resources may be increased through *altered chords, modulation, interchangeability of modes* (bi-modality), and *secondary function*.

Example 155

Excerpt, *Insbruck, ich muss dich lassen*, Heinrich Isaac (1450–1517)

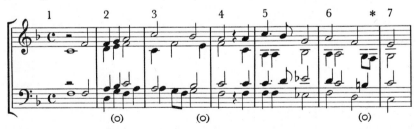

Isaac's concern for line and color seems to account for the reordering of the spacing in measures 5–7, where the tenor sings consistently above the alto. This procedure, which may apply to any or all voices, is called *crossed voices*.

It is recalled that pitch resources of the fifteenth and sixteenth centuries emanated from the church modes; therefore the Isaac progression would be typically denoted as *modal succession*. The

111

modal characteristics are ionian, transposed to F. There is an indication, however, that most of the chords relate specifically to a central, or tonic, triad. These relationships, when systematically employed, create what is termed *functional harmony* (tonal progression). Usually, this descriptive term is reserved for progressions derived from a major or minor tonality or key.

DIMINISHED TRIADS

Isaac's song is comprised of major and minor sonorities and, at three points, of *diminished triads*, marked (o). Built of two consecutive minor thirds, the diminished triad occurs as a result of scale formations on the seventh degree in major and minor keys (vii°) and on the second degree in a minor key (ii°). Cadential use of the diminished sound predates the tertian period, while its utilization in the late Renaissance is for the purpose of lending occasional color. The diminished chord is found in root position and in second inversion, but the most frequent usage of any diminished triad is as a chord of first inversion.

Chord root and fifth have strong tendencies to resolve to a third, for example, B–F to C–E; the inner tone of the triad remains neutral, free to move in either direction, by step or by leap. For acoustical reasons, it is advisable to *double the third of the chord*. In practice it is observed, however, that the fifth is frequently doubled. This facilitates part-writing, while accomplishing the resolution of the tritone. The chord root, often the leading tone of a scale, is the least preferred doubling.

Example 156

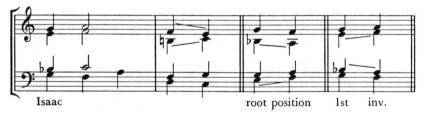

Isaac   root position   1st   inv.

In the creation of new and viable sound, composers have devised several concepts which expand the diatonic resources of the modal and tonal systems:

Altered chords

Sonorities which utilize one or more tones foreign to a given scale are frequently referred to as *altered chords*. In the Renaissance and Baroque periods, with the exception of the Gesualdos (the experimenters with chromaticism), altered chords are not an especially common phenomenon; rather, a tone which requires an accidental more often denotes one of the following:

A change of tonality
A change from major to minor (or the reverse)
A change in the function of the chord

Modulation   *Modulation* is a process which achieves a change of tonality. The change may be effected by rhythmic, melodic, or harmonic factors. Depending upon its behavior, the modulation is called *transient* or *permanent*.

Modulations are also categorized according to the kind of change that is used to relate one tonal area to another; according to this categorization, they are usually called diatonic, chromatic, or enharmonic modulations. Example 157 illustrates a *diatonic*, or *common chord*, modulation. The simple prerequisite for a diatonic modulation is one triad which is found, unaltered, in both the old and new keys. As an example, the triads CEG, DFA, FAC, ACE, and BDF are *common* to the diatonic scale resources of C major and A harmonic minor.

Example 157

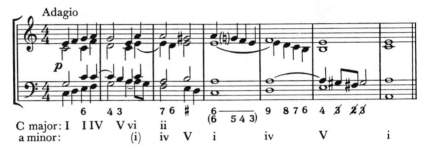

Normally, a distinction is made between a change in tonal center and a change from major to minor, or vice versa, using parallel relationships. The former is a true modulation (Example 157), while the latter is simply a *change of mode* (Example 158):

Example 158

A modulation may augment the original harmonic resources by as much as a hundred percent, depending on the choice of the new key. Example 159 illustrates four relationships, from a possible total of twenty-two.

Example 159

a. Original resources in C major
b. Added resources from A harmonic minor (submediant relationship)
c. Added resources from G major (dominant relationship)
d. New resources from C♯ major (chromatic relationship)

NOTE: Chromatic and enharmonic modulation will be discussed in
a subsequent chapter.

Bi-modality   The practice of employing chords from the parallel relationship
(Example 158) is commonly observed. Two terms are used synony-
mously for this concept: *interchangeability of modes*, and *bi-modality*.
In some eras, and with certain composers, the bi-modal relationships
are prominent. The increase in harmonic resources is shown in
Example 160:

Example 160

a. Original resources from C major
b. New resources from *harmonic minor*, parallel relation

Related to the bi-modal concept is the mannerism of substituting
a major tonic triad at cadence points within a minor-key framework.
This device, Example 161, is referred to as a *Picardy third*:

Example 161

**SECONDARY
FUNCTION**   One of the most important concepts in theory—one crucial to the
understanding and analysis of chordal relationship—is that of
secondary function. The concept provides for the momentary borrow-
ing of resources which relate to scale degrees other than the tonic.

From its inception and earliest practice, the preponderance of secondary function has been directed to the dominant level: V of V, or vii° of V. (An early example, by whatever name, occurs in the Isaac song, Example 155, marked *.) Example 162 lists the most common relationships involving secondary function:

Example 162

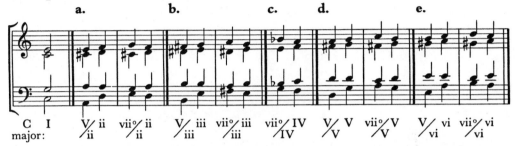

Tonality and musical continuity are in no way destroyed by the use of secondary function. The concept establishes an accurate description of musical function; its use allows for a momentary emphasis of a diatonic chord other than the tonic and secures additional resources within any given tonality. The augmented resources are illustrated in Example 163:

Example 163

a. Original resources from C major
b. New resources from *secondary dominants* and from *secondary leading tones*

Chromatic inflections frequently relate to secondary function or bimodal interchange, or a combination of both.

EMBELLISHING TONES

An entire category of non-chord tones has a musical function which is primarily that of decoration and embellishment. These include the *cambiata, changing tones, neighboring* (or *auxiliary*) *tones, escape tone,* and *appoggiatura*.

Cambiata

The cambiata (It. *cambiare,* to change or exchange) is an ornamental figuration used with great frequency in the sixteenth century. The *nota cambiata* moves by leap in the same direction as the basic harmonic progression; characteristically, it moves too far and must retreat step-wise in the opposite direction for its resolution (Example 164):

Example 164

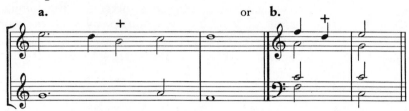

Changing tones

Changing tones may be considered as a possible development of the same figuration. The chord tone is embellished by the notes immediately above and below (or the reverse order) in a step-leap-step pattern. Changing tones may be accompanied by a new chord at the point of resolution; they may be diatonic or chromatic, according to the considerations of style (Example 165):

Example 165

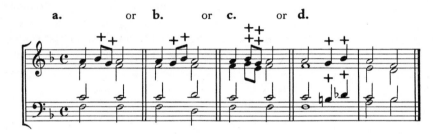

**Neighboring
tones**

Of less complexity, neighboring tones (neighbor tones, auxiliary tones, auxiliaries) are closely related to changing tones. In any given voice, a chord tone is embellished—above or below—by a single non-harmonic note. A neighboring tone may be diatonic or chromatic, although it is not common practice to inflect the third of the chord (Example 166):

Example 166

Escape tone

The escape tone or *échappée* is the reverse of the cambiata; i.e., it is approached by step in the direction opposite to that of the basic progression, then turns and resolves by leap (Example 167):

Example 167

Appoggiatura

A final, and somewhat controversial, embellishing tone, is the appoggiatura (It. *appoggiare*, to lean). One of the few areas of agreement among writers concerning the appoggiatura is that it is rhythmically strong; i.e., the dissonance is on the strong part of the beat. Two principal interpretations of the term are listed below:

1. A non-harmonic tone on the rhythmically strong part of the beat which resolves step-wise to a chord tone on the weak part of the beat (Example 168a, b).
2. A non-harmonic tone approached by leap and resolving, typically, step-wise down (Example 168c, d).

Example 168

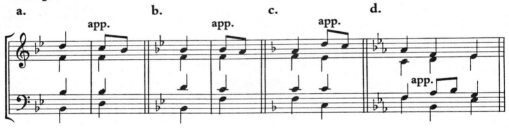

Observations:

1. The appoggiatura may occur in any voice, although it is perhaps most striking when used in an exposed upper voice.
2. *Appoggiature* are observed in all eras. In the eighteenth and nineteenth centuries simultaneous *appoggiature* form what is commonly referred to as an *appoggiatura chord*.

It is typical that embellishing tones of all varieties, with the exception of the appoggiatura, are *rhythmically weak*.

SUGGESTED
STUDIES

1. Analyze Example 169 in the following terms:
   The rhythmic-melodic factors of organization
   The root movement of chords
   The relationship of each chord to the tonal axes G and B♮
   The identification of all non-chord tones
   The musical organization as a whole in terms of unification and diversity

Example 169

Measures 1–18, *Ave Verum Corpus*, William Byrd (1543–1623)

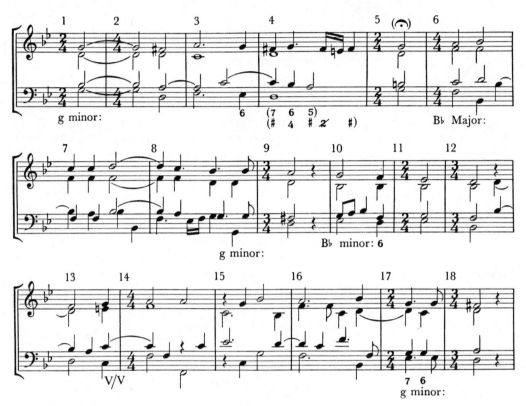

2. Composition and invention:

    a. Using Example 170, invent two inner voices to the given soprano and figured bass.

Example 170

From John Dowland (1562–1626)

b. In Example 171, add the three upper voices to the given figured bass. Add an harmonic analysis. Invent a complementary phrase; repeat the original phrase.

Example 171

Adapted from Orlando Gibbons (1583–1625)

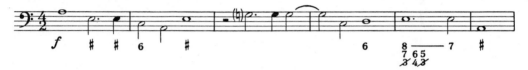

c. In Example 172, add three lower voices to the given soprano and numerals. (All notes marked + are to be treated as non-chord tones.)

Example 172

From Michael Praetorius (1571–1621)

d. In G major (*allegro*, duple meter), invent a four-voice piece from the given Roman numerals:

I IV$_6$ V I$_6$ ii$_6$ V vi IV V
V/vi vi V$_6$ I IV ii V I
IV$_6$ V$_{4323}$ I ||

e. Compose a short original composition (about 14 measures) using the concepts and vocabulary that have been introduced in Chapter 16.

17

THE SIX-FOUR CHORD
THE AUGMENTED TRIAD
HARMONIC RHYTHM

THE SIX-FOUR CHORD

This passage from Morley's *Agnus Dei* (Example 173) is an exciting combination of the modal and tonal systems. The linear emphasis does not preclude harmonic clarity; viable rhythms do not impede the quiet and consistent motion; predictability and surprise are coequals.

Observe that in measures 5 and 6 Morley continues to employ a series of sixth chords (i.e., a latter-day *fauxbourdon*). A triad whose *fifth* is in the bass is denoted as a *six-four chord*: $^6_4$ (see measures 2 and 8).

Example 173

Final 9 measures, *Agnus Dei*, Thomas Morley (1557–1602)

Morley's excerpt contains two such sonorities, each employed in a precise manner. Unlike the unrestricted employment of root position and first inversion chords, the use of the six-four chord has been specific and selective. Four of the most common uses are cited in Example 174:

Example 174

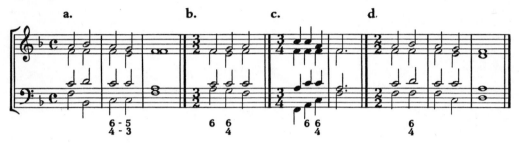

a. *Cadential six-four*: as its name implies, this usage is most often found at points of cadence; the usual behavior is for 6 to move to 5 in the same voice while 4 moves to 3, also in the same voice.

b. *Passing six-four*: often observed in a rhythmically weak position in the measure, the passing six-four is primarily melodic in function; it is particularly appropriate when the outside voices move in conjunct contrary motion.

c. *Arpeggiated (or chordal) six-four*: appropriate for keyboard or instrumental music, the arpeggiated six-four is simply a chord outline, melodically deployed.

d. *Stationary six-four*: derived from the melodic motion of two upper neighboring tones

Doubling

With few exceptions, practice of composers has consistently doubled the *bass* note, the fifth of the triad.

Function and restricted use

A triad in second inversion is apt to change or negate its basic function. For example, the *function* of all of measure 2, Example 174a, is dominant, with the upper voices a^i f^i behaving as non-chord tones to g^i e^i. In Examples 174b, c, d, the six-four chords are decidely weak, approaching a kind of non-function. More than any other triadic formation, the six-four sonority poses serious musical problems. Its utilization, in initial studies, should be severely restricted.

THE AUGMENTED TRIAD

The five-voice texture of the Tomkins anthem (Example 175) provides for a rich contrapuntal fabric. Imitation (measures 4–6) and a tenor pedal (measures 4–7) are compositional devices which assist in the unfolding of musical content. In two instances, marked *,

Example 175

Final 7 measures, *O Lord, I have loved,* Thomas Tomkins (1572–1656)

harmonic tension is heightened by the use of *augmented triads* in an otherwise major–minor environment.

Of the four kinds of triads, the augmented triad (★) has been the least frequently utilized. It is not formed from any of the modes and its solitary natural occurrence is on the third degree of the harmonic minor scale, III+. Even in this possible context it is primarily a melodic, not an harmonic, phenomenon.

Example 176

g harmonic minor: I ii° III⁺ iv V VI vii°

*Most typically III appears as a *major* triad in the minor mode.

The relatively late appearance of the harmonic minor scale, the unusual dissonance of the two overlapping major thirds, and the weakness of the augmented triad in terms of function, are factors that have conspired against its frequent use.

Tomkin's augmented triads are the result of linear motivations. Reduced to four parts, these are shown in simpler, but essential, form in Example 177:

Example 177

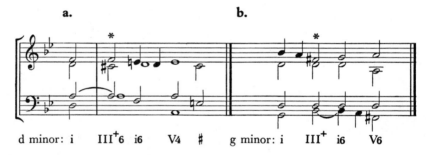

d minor: i III⁺6 i6 V4 ♯ g minor: i III⁺ i6 V6

Functions

In Example 177a, the III⁺ (*) functions as a dominant with the suspended fⁱ moving conclusively to eⁱ. In Example 177b, the III⁺ functions as an embellished tonic with fⁱ♯ moving to gⁱ.

Doubling

The *third* of the augmented triad is most commonly doubled; the chord root is occasionally doubled, depending upon the context and behavior.

With the inclusion of the augmented sonority, the triadic vocabulary—without expansion—is completed. These four basic dispositions with their inversions served as the basic materials of the *familiar*, or chordal, style of the fifteenth and sixteenth centuries.

HARMONIC RHYTHM

Harmonic rhythm is a term used to describe the frequency of chord change in a composition. Example 178a–c shows the same melody harmonized in three different ways.

a. A *slow* harmonic rhythm indicates infrequent chord changes, as this extreme example shows.

Example 178

a.   b.

c.

b. A *moderate* harmonic rhythm is achieved by chord changes on some—but not all—of the given melodic notes.

c. A *fast* harmonic rhythm involves a chord change for each note (or nearly so) of the melody.

Determination of tempo

Most Renaissance and Baroque scores have been inherited without tempo indications. Performance practice of this music depends, then, on tradition—if one exists—and on the musicologists' investigations of the period. Often harmonic rhythm, together with the medium (voices, keyboard, an instrumental ensemble), give the best musical clues in determining an appropriate tempo.

Although personal taste is both inevitable and desirable, common agreement would probably establish the following general tempi, as applied to Example 178a-c:

a. Allegro
b. Moderato
c. Andante to Adagio

Arbitrarily, Example 178c could be marked *Presto*, of course, but the effect, particularly if intended for voices, would be curious and quite detrimental to its natural implications. Any determination of tempo must consider: clarity of the lines and sonorities in performance, and the ability of the sounds to project acoustically. In vocal music, a foremost factor is the character of the text; in instrumental music the performer must rely on consensus or reason—or ideally, both.

SUGGESTED
STUDIES

1. Invent inner voices for the given soprano and figured bass in Example 179. Provide an harmonic analysis and identify all cadences.

Example 179

Adapted from Guillaume Costeley (1531–1606)

2. Invent three upper voices to the given figured bass in Example 180. Provide an harmonic analysis.

Example 180

Adapted from Orlandus Lassus (1532–1594)

3. Compose a four-voice composition from the Roman and Arabic numerals given below:

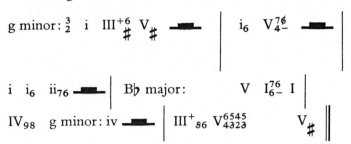

g minor: $\frac{3}{2}$ i III$^{+6}_{\sharp}$ V$_{\sharp}$ — | i$_6$ V$^{7\flat}_{4-}$ — |

i i$_6$ ii$_{76}$ — | B♭ major: V I$^{76}_{6-}$ I |

IV$_{98}$ g minor: iv — | III$^+{}_{56}$ V$^{6545}_{4323}$ V$_{\sharp}$ ‖

18

MELODIC WRITING (FIFTEENTH
AND SIXTEENTH CENTURIES)

HARMONIC TEXTURES IN THREE,
FIVE, AND SIX VOICES

RHYTHMIC CONTROL

MELODIC WRITING (FIFTEENTH AND SIXTEENTH CENTURIES)

Examples 181–186 serve to illustrate several common characteristics of melodic writing in the fifteenth and sixteenth centuries. The six excerpts, both vocal and instrumental, contain a variety of musical gestures, yet similar controls of pitch and duration are evident:

1. Phrases often begin with long note values; rhythmically modulate to shorter values; and, of course, arrive at a point of repose. What one observes here is a fundamental axiom of music and life that insists that every living organism be endowed with a beginning, a middle, and an end.
2. Each phrase contains a balance of conjunct and disjunct motion.
3. Intervals of a fourth or larger typically change direction after the leap. (Observe the arrows of Examples 181–183.) Similarly, a scalar passage which encompasses a perfect fourth, fifth, or octave will point back to the generating note. (Observe the arrows of Example 184.)
4. Usually a phrase has only one high point, dramatically placed to achieve vitality and a musical *event* within the line.

Example 185, by Gabrieli, is remarkable for its rhythmic balance and symmetry. Example 186, typical of the works of Gesualdo, introduces here a passage of chromaticism from one of the most adventuresome composers in history. Although some features of Gesualdo's melodic writing relate clearly to sixteenth-century procedures, the totality is somewhat outside the mainstream of high Renaissance musical practice.

Stylistic differences among composers of this era tended to be minimized—resulting in a kind of universal vocabulary. Nonetheless, the selective processes of individual composers have obviously always differed.

128

Example 181

From *Mille Regretz*, Josquin des Prez (1450–1521)

Mil - le re - grettz - - - - - de vous ha - ban-don-ner

Example 182

From *Kyrie Eleison*, Tomás Luis de Victoria (c. 1549–1611)

Ky - ri - e e - - lei - son Ky-rie___ e - - - lei - son

Example 183

From *Missa Papae Marcelli*, Giovanni Pierluigi da Palestrina (1524–1594)

Ag — - nus De - - - - - - i

Example 184

From *Contrapuntal Study*, Jan. P. Sweelinck (1562–1621)

Example 185

From *Ricercare del 12° tono*, Andrea Gabrieli (1510–1586)

Example 186

From Madrigal, *Moro lasso*, Carlo Gesualdo (1560–1613)

**HARMONIC
TEXTURES IN
THREE, FIVE,
AND SIX VOICES**

Although initial harmonic studies tend to emphasize the manipulation of four voices, an examination and use of other textures should be considered an important part of the student's musical experience. Each line of these five measures (Example 187) contributes a melodic and rhythmic dimension. Harmonically, this chorus is effected from six different triads, all in root position. Each sonority contains one root, third, and fifth, with the exception of those chords marked X.

**Three-voice
texture**

Example 187

Excerpt from the *St. John Passion*, William Byrd (1543-1623)

Omission of fifth

In these instances, the fifth of the chord is typically omitted. Byrd's example would indicate that a majority of the chords without fifths contain two roots and one third. Occasionally, a sonority contains one root and two thirds (marked ^X_X)—probably for reasons of voice leading. The fifth of a triad, while contributing to the fullness of sound, is obviously the least essential member of a chord and may therefore be omitted if part-writing or control of line so necessitate.

**Five-voice
texture**

The effect of the chord fifth in a five- or six-voice texture is quite unobtrusive. Example 188 contains ten instances of a doubled fifth—two roots, one third, two fifths. All other sonorities contain a triple root; in this example one does not observe a doubled third.

Example 188

From *Ballett (My Bonny Lass)*, Thomas Morley (1557-1602)

**Six-voice
texture**

Example 189 is an extraction of accented sonorities within a polyphonic texture, as observed in the Agnus Dei I of Palestrina's *Pope Marcellus Mass*. A majority of sonorities contain three roots; thirds and fifths are rather equally distributed. It is important to observe, however, that the chord third, functioning as a leading tone ($f\sharp^i$ in measure 1), remains undoubled.

Example 189

**RHYTHMIC
CONTROL**

A feature of some polyphonic music of the fifteenth and sixteenth
centuries is its continual rhythmic flow. (As a reminder—music of
this period was notated without bar lines; therefore the phrase
structure of each line was determined by the text or by a clearly
defined point of repose). Two concepts are observed, both of which
retain their validity to the present time:

1. *Composite rhythm*: this results from the vertical combination of
   the several lines
2. *Overlapping phrases*: these effect a rhythmic control devoid of
   stoppage and angularity, and were a major feature of style.

Example 190

Example 190 illustrates these typical sixteenth-century practices. (Brackets indicate phrase structure.)

Consideration of these rhythmic concepts, applied where appropriate to the chordal style, will assist in achieving a total musicality.

SUGGESTED
STUDIES

1. Write a single-line composition of about 14 measures on the text *Kyrie Eleison* (or a similar text), using mode, range, intervals, and rhythm appropriate for the late sixteenth century.

2. Write a three-voice composition, using the melody in Example 191 as the upper voice.

Example 191

Attributed to Thomas Tallis (1515–1585)

3. Realize the figured bass in Example 192 in *five* parts; invent a consequent phrase.

Example 192

4. Prepare an analysis of *D'une Coline* (Example 193) in the following terms:

The meaning of *vers mesuré*; the special metric-rhythmic features of this work

A comparison of three- and five-part texture to four-part writing

The design of the composition

The extent and type of repetition

The shape of each line; the kinds of motion between the outside voices

The root movement

The use of secondary function

The use of bi-modality

Identification of non-harmonic tones

The relationship of this analysis to performance

Example 193

D'une Coline, Claude le Jeune (1528–1600)

Reprise à 5

Je la voy de loin, Et je l'ai – me fort, Je la veu cueil- lir,

Et la main j'y tens, Mais las c'est en vain.

19

CHORDAL ACCOMPANIMENT

CHORDS OF THE SEVENTH

DOMINANT SEVENTH

AUGMENTED SECOND

THE TRITONE

CHORDAL ACCOMPANIMENT

Of particular importance to harmonic syntax were the innovative practices of secular music. Noteworthy is a large repertory for voice and lute, in which an essentially chordal accompaniment supports a solo melody. Compiled in 1574, *The Bottegari Lutebook*[1] is one of the most rewarding collections of the late Renaissance. The 132 compositions, by several leading composers, would indicate that "singing to the lute" formed an important genre of court entertainment and musical media.

Example 194

No. 54, *Aria da Stanza*, Cosimo Bottegari (1554–1620)

From *The Bottegari Lutebook* (Wellesley Edition No. 8, 1965), ed. Carol MacClintock. Used by permission.

[1] Edited by Carol MacClintock (Wellesley, Mass.: Wellesley Edition No. 8, 1965).

- ti,   Voi che do -na - sti a   duo' begl' oc - ch'il   co - re,   *senza*
- ti   Far pa - le - se   non   pass' il suo do - lo - re,   *ripresa*
- ti   Non si muo-v'a pie - tà   di chi si   mo - re: *seguita*
- to   Ea - man-d'al-trui, non   es - ser punto A - ma - to.   *da*
                                                                         capo

Observations:

1. The slightly asymmetrical (5 plus 3) *Aria* satisfies all tonal requirements, with the possible exception of the chord marked X, which
   serves as a leading-tone triad to A♭.
2. Both phrases conclude with authentic cadences: in measure 5 to
   A♮ major; in measure 8 to f minor.
3. The usual avoidance of parallel perfect fifths and octaves is
   relaxed in favor of characteristic lute chordal dispositions.
4. The non-agreement of key signature with the actual tonal orientation is quite typical of this collection and of the practice of this
   era.

Monteverdi's *Lament* for solo voice and basso continuo (Example
195) ideally illustrates a declamatory style of the early Baroque
period. (The text, omitted here, describes moments of personal
tragedy.)

Observations:

1. The metric and rhythmic freedoms provide for non-predictability;
   at the same time the reiteration of certain pitches effects irregular
   groupings in time.

Example 195

Excerpt from *Lamento d'Olimpia*, Claudio Monteverdi (c. 1567–1643)

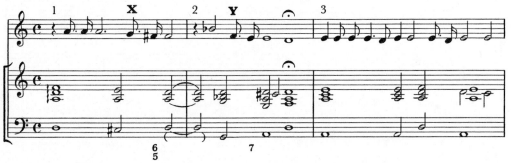

2. The structure of the two phrases is asymmetrical, distributed at a ratio of 10 half-notes to 22 half-notes. Balance and unity are achieved, however, by a repetition (with variant) of the most poignant melodic figure. (Compare measure 2 to measure 6.)

In reduction to its essential pitches, the melodic motion of these measures may be represented as follows:

Example 196

Observe that the melodic contour and the placement of primary and secondary high points and low points is carefully controlled. The motion is often disjunct, achieving definition and accent for specific notes and words. There are two *tonal axes*: D (measures 1–2 and 5–6) and A (measure 3). Measure 4, which is central in terms of time-span, is transient in C and accomplishes the return to D.

**CHORDS OF
THE SEVENTH**

Slow-moving triadic harmonies are enriched, in four instances, by the addition of *chordal sevenths* (marked X and Y in Example 195). The presence of the seventh in Western music was typically a result of linearity up to the time of Monteverdi; thereafter, the chord gradually emerges as an independent, clearly defined harmonic entity.

An additional third may be added to any triad, forming a seventh with the root (Example 197).

Example 197

Seven chords of different *color* or *quality* are derived from the major
and harmonic minor scales. Although terminology varies, a logical
nomenclature identifies first the triad quality (major, minor, diminished, augmented), and second, the distance from the chord root to
the seventh (major, minor, diminished, augmented).

	Triad	Seventh
1.	Major	Major
2.	Minor	Major
3.	Minor	Minor
4.	Diminished	Minor
5.	Minor	Minor
6.	Augmented	Major
7.	Major	Major
8.	Minor	Minor
9.	Major	Minor
10.	Minor	Minor
11.	Major	Major
12.	Diminished	Minor
13.	Diminished	Diminished

Obviously, these seventh-chords, which result from the diatonic
scales, are the most frequently used. Others are observed especially
in the nineteenth century, both in practice and in theory:

Example 198

Observe in Example 198b that, although c^i and $b\sharp^i$ are octave
equivalents, in equal temperament, their functions differ.

**DOMINANT
SEVENTH**

Throughout the seventeenth and eighteenth centuries, certain
qualities of seventh chords were more frequently employed than
others. The triad with seventh, built on the fifth scale degree, common
to both major and minor modes, is typically the most prominent. A
general hierarchy of usage would perhaps have the following order:

1. Major–Minor
2. Diminished–Minor
3. Minor–Minor
4. Diminished–Diminished
5. Major–Major

Other qualities are used for special effect or in chromatic contexts.

**Dominant seventh
as secondary
function**

Since the addition of the seventh does not alter the triad function, seventh chords are frequently employed as secondary function.

Example 199

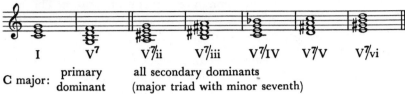

C major: primary dominant — all secondary dominants (major triad with minor seventh)

Example 200

c minor:

**Major-minor
seventh from
alteration**

An additional occurrence of this sonority is found on the fourth scale degree of the minor mode. Its introduction was prompted, perhaps, by consideration of scale (melodic minor), or by mechanical reasons—the avoidance of the melodic interval of an augmented second (Example 201).

Example 201

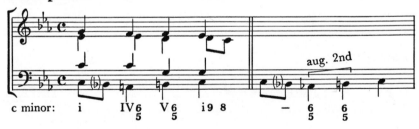

Figured bass symbols for all seventh chords are illustrated below:

**Figured bass
symbols**

Example 202

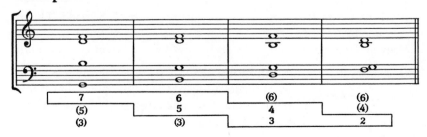

The pattern $7 - \frac{6}{5} - \frac{4}{3} - 2$ is a convenient memory guide. (In place of the 2, some theorists prefer to use $\frac{4}{2}$, which distinguishes this inversion more clearly from a 2-1 suspension figure.)

Preparation and resolution

Since the initial use of sevenths resulted from linearity, it is reasonable to observe that the *preparation* and *resolution* of chordal sevenths are based upon melodic considerations. The terminology used to describe these procedures unfortunately borrows from non-harmonic-tone nomenclature.

Preparation: as passing-tone figure
           as upper-auxiliary figure
           as suspension figure
           as appoggiatura figure

Example 203

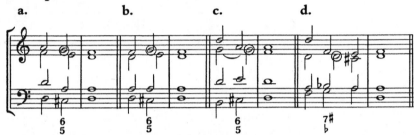

Resolution: the usual resolution of any minor seventh, irrespective of inversion, is *step-wise down*.

In practice there are, fortunately, non-conformists. "Irregular" (more accurately, "less usual") resolutions are illustrated in the following examples from the works of two rather successful composers (Example 204):

Example 204

d minor: i   ii°$\frac{6}{5}$ V$\frac{4}{2}$ VI

a. Monteverdi. Resolutions made for reasons of linearity and mode.

b. J. S. Bach. The melodic figure in the bass takes precedence over typical resolution.

Dissolution

A common behavior pattern for the seventh is that of common-tone absorption into the subsequent harmony. A distinction is sometimes made by referring to this behavior as *dissolution* (Example 205).

Example 205

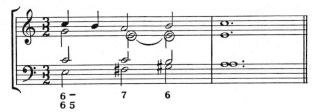

$$
\begin{matrix}
6 - \\
6\ 5 \qquad\qquad 7 \qquad\qquad 6
\end{matrix}
$$

Third inversion

The *third inversion* ($\frac{4}{2}$) of any seventh chord may be approached, employed, and resolved in the ways illustrated in Example 203. However, there are two very frequent and additional uses which are illustrated below (Example 206).

Convergence of thirds

In Example 207 the organizational feature, in terms of harmony, is the *convergence of two sets of thirds*—yielding in the approach to cadence. Doublings, resolution of chord sevenths, and perhaps even the resolution of melodic dissonances, are all of secondary considera-

Example 206:

Example 207

From *Salmo a 4 voci ed organo*, Claudio Monteverdi

*Accidentals appearing above the notes are not contained in the original manuscript, but are suggested by most editors. In this instance, however, their inclusion would detract from the premise of convergence of major triads. Further, the two suggested B♭'s in the tenor line (measures 2, 4) create melodically an augmented second and an unresolved augmented fourth, respectively.

tion. As a result, melodic and harmonic independence is achieved, producing a passage of singular beauty. This compositional procedure is again rather frequently encountered in the works of certain twentieth-century composers.

AUGMENTED SECOND

In vocal music of all periods prior to the nineteenth century, the melodic interval of an *augmented second* is typically avoided.

Example 208

a.   **b.** Normal doubling   **c.** Doubled third in VI

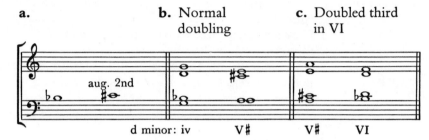

THE TRITONE
(Augmented fourth, diminished fifth)

Two other intervals with the common name of *tritone* require cautious voice leading: the augmented fourth and the diminished fifth.

Example 209

a. Melodic   **b.** Harmonic **c.** Melodic   **d.** Harmonic

The augmented fourth *expands* in normal resolution   The diminshed fifth *contracts* in normal resolution

Several centuries of musical and theoretical controversy on the tritone has given the *Diabolus in Musica* a rather special reputation. Its *harmonic* use in the seventeenth and eighteenth centuries is not uncommon, however.

Example 210

a. *Von Gott will ich nicht lassen*, J. S. Bach   **b.** *Was mein Gott will,* J. S. Bach

1. Complete Example 211 to five parts (close structure). Comment briefly on each of the following items:
   The phrase structure
   The types of cadences
   The implied tonal orientation (level) at each cadence
   The kinds of root movement

Example 211

Exultent Caeli, Claudio Monteverdi

*Sharp added to signature, note values halved.

2. Complete Example 212 to four parts. Include an harmonic analysis.

Example 212

3. Continue the realization of the given figured bass in Example 213 with three or four voices.

Example 213

Solo recitative from *Orfeo*, Claudio Monteverdi

4. Analyze and be able to discuss the given passage from *Orfeo* of Monteverdi (Example 214) in the following terms:
   The meaning of *Ritornello*
   The kinds of root movement
   The kinds of non-harmonicism
   The extent and kind of repetition
   The kinds of compositional devices

Example 214

Excerpt from *Orfeo*, Claudio Monteverdi

5. Compose an accompaniment (keyboard, lute, or guitar) for the following solo line (Example 215). Use Example 195 as a model.

Example 215

No. 53, *Aria da Stanza*, Cosimo Bottegari

From *The Bottegari Lutebook* (Wellesley Edition No. 8, 1965), ed. Carol MacClintock. Used by permission.

PART III
The Completed Major-Minor System

"Mortal men live by mutual exchange."
— *Lucretius*

20

CHORD CLASSIFICATIONS
GROUND BASS
AUGMENTED SIXTH CHORDS
KEYBOARD REALIZATIONS
NEAPOLITAN SIXTH CHORD

The major-minor system became firmly established in the first half of the seventeenth century. Tonal progression supplanted modal succession; harmonic function became synonymous with musical organization; non-harmonicism and modulation, in the modern meaning of these terms, were employed consistently and with a full knowledge of their theoretical and musical significance.

Observation of Baroque harmonic practice reveals a system which is governed principally by root movement by perfect fifth. Implied in the system are the specific relationships of all diatonic triads to a central tonic chord.

Example 216

CHORD
CLASSIFICA-
TIONS

Example 216 illustrates a series of relationships, or *chord classifications*, to a given tonic:

First relationship (classification): the dominant and leading-tone triads are the most closely related to the tonic—in terms of *function* (effected by the presence of the raised seventh degree of the scale and, in the case of the dominant, a root whose distance from the tonic is a perfect fifth)

Second relationship: ii (ii°) and IV (iv)

Third relationship: vi (VI)

Fourth relationship: iii (III or III⁺)

In progressing from the most distantly related sonority to the tonic, one may establish a chain of fifths in root movement:

Example 217

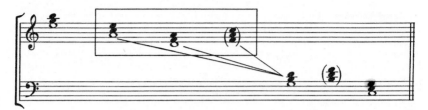

II, IV, VI often have a common function—that of dominant prefix or "approach chord." Baroque composers certainly did not indulge in an endless series of iii, vi, ii, V, I progressions—although analyses of the substructure of compositions of this period indicate a strong reliance on set relationships. Modifications in the chain of fifths were fortunately numerous, and include:

1. Omission of a relationship, e.g.
     I   vi——V   I, or
     I   iii——IV——I
2. Alteration of a chord or the use of secondary function
3. Tonal variation achieved by modulation
4. Use of only one or two relationships—common throughout the Baroque and Classical periods—
     I   V   I   V   I, or
     I   IV   V   I   ii   V   I
   as well as use of the infinite combinations which are a part of invention.

Example 218 illustrates the basic system as well as the modifications. In this famous recitative and aria, other important Baroque concepts and compositional procedures may be observed. The recitative is supported by a keyboard part in which the performer made certain decisions regarding position and deployment of chords, but within the harmonic confines indicated by the composer. Observe that the essential shape of the line is downward from c^{ii} to d^{i} and accomplishes a modulation from c minor to g minor.

GROUND BASS   The aria, or lament, is constructed on a *ground bass*. Purcell's five-measure series (measures 1–5, Example 218) is an example of the bass patterns used in the Baroque period as a foundation and unification for through-composed variations—specifically, the *chaconne* and *passacaglia*. The pattern, Example 219, has an interesting division into two parts: three consecutive.pairs of descending semi-tones, followed by a counter-thrust in the opposite direction. The corresponding change in rhythm (marked XX) provides an element of non-predictability.

Example 218

Excerpt from *Dido and Aeneas*, Henry Purcell (c. 1659–1695)

Pub. Novello & Co., Ltd.

Example 219

The relationship of the ground bass to the vocal line is subtle; the descending semi-tones are somewhat concealed by rhythmic shift:

Example 220

Observe the poignant word-painting by the use of the tritone for "trouble" in measure 11 of Example 218. Example 218 illustrates three different versions, or treatments, of the ground bass:

Without harmonization, marked X
First harmonization, marked Y
Second or altered harmonization, marked Z

These harmonic variants are most important as a musical consideration, for the procedure effects a change of musical environment for
the constant reiteration of the bass pattern. The first harmonization
illustrates two forms of dominant (measure 6) and two forms of
subdominant (measure 7).

**Cadential
formula**

The cadence in measures 9–10 (ii$^6_5$ i$^6_4$ V i) is a cadential formula of
unusual durability—used quite consistently by composers for nearly
two hundred years.

Example 221

a. Purcell

b. Common four-voice
disposition

$$ii°\,^6_5 \quad i\,6 \atop 4 \quad V\sharp \quad i$$

**AUGMENTED
SIXTH CHORDS**

The final measure of Purcell's recitative employs a sonority of unusual quality which includes the melodic interval of an *augmented
sixth*:

Example 222

Augmented sixth sonorities have an extended and interesting history,
observed from about the time of Gesualdo in the sixteenth century.
In the Baroque and Classical periods, augmented sixths were used
sparingly at points of musical tension and decidedly in a linear context; usage in the Romantic period became frequent to the point
where entire compositions were built around this focal sonority.
Conversely, its absence from most twentieth-century scores is
conspicuous.

Three most common formations of augmented sixth chords are

shown below. Other, less frequently used forms are shown at a later point in the text.

Example 223

a. Italian   **b.** German   **c.** French

These three forms share common properties:

1. All are typically found in a minor key.
2. All employ the *raised fourth degree* of the scale.
3. All have the same harmonic function, either as iv (Italian and German) or ii (French).
4. All contain unclassified triads (i.e., spellings other than major, minor, augmented, or diminished); for example: C♯E♭ G or A C♯ E♭ G.
5. The resolution of the augmented sixth interval typically expands to the octave; the German sixth chord (IV$^6_5$) typically resolves to a tonic $^6_4$ to avoid parallel perfect fifths.

Example 224

During the Classical and Romantic periods, modification of the behavior of augmented sixth chords is noticeable:

Example 225

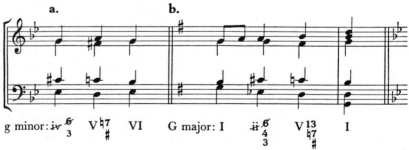

g minor: i $\quad$ V$^7_\sharp$ $\quad$ iv$^6_5$ $\quad$ =V$^{\flat7}$

A$\flat$ major:I$^{\flat6}$ $\quad$ IV $\quad$ V $\quad$ I

NOTE: The raised fourth degree may be employed for other chords—
i.e., non-augmented sixth chords—especially vii°^{7} of V. For example,
in g minor: C$\sharp$E$\natural$ GB$\flat$ = vii°^{7}/V.

a. "Irregular" (less usual) resolutions
b. Appearance in a major key
c. Enharmonic spellings used for modulation to distant keys

**KEYBOARD
REALIZATIONS**
Corelli's *Concerto* (Example 226) is illustrative of the Baroque
composer's interest in contrasts: the formal design of the entire
concerto is a series of alternating slow and fast sections; the instrumental contrast is provided by a group of soloists (It. *concertino*, con-
certed) and a larger and reinforced group (It. *ripieno*, full) which
engage each other in a constant dialogue.

An interesting feature of this concerto is that the *ripieno* parts may
be omitted, leaving a perfectly formed *trio sonata* from the remaining
concertino parts. In this modern edition, the cembalo (organ or
harpsichord) has been realized from the figured bass of the concertino.

Observations:

1. A consistent three- to four-voice texture is maintained, with all
   notes of the chords strictly conforming to the composer's figured
   bass instructions.
2. The actual placement (*disposition*) of the notes is at the discretion
   of the keyboard performer who, in this example, uses a combination of
   a. doubling of string parts
   b. providing for filler between the two violins and the violon-
      cello
3. The cembalo part has no real rhythmic independence and effects
   an unobtrusive supporting sound for the strings.

The realization of Corelli's *Concerto* may be taken as quite representative of current editions and performance practice today. One
imagines, however, that at an actual eighteenth-century performance
—in the hands of a virtuoso keyboard artist—the figured bass realiza-

Example 226

Concerto V, Op. 6, No. 5, Arcangelo Corelli (1653–1713); cembalo
realization by Waldemar Woehl

Reprinted from Peters Edition Nr. 4485.

tion would have been far more independent, embellished, and
elaborate in general.

Improvisation is one of several concerns or interests shared by the
eighteenth- and twentieth-century composer. For a revealing insight
into improvisatory performance practice, the student is asked to
compare a popular song chord chart with any recorded or live version.
One questions whether the *intent* of improvisation has really changed
substantially in the past two hundred years.

**NEAPOLITAN
SIXTH CHORD**

Measure 12 of the Corelli example (Example 226) contains still another interesting sonority, involving an alteration of a diatonic scale degree. The *Neapolitan sixth chord* derives part of its name from the fact that its early appearance was almost exclusively as a chord of first inversion (6).

Observations concerning the Neapolitan sixth include:

1. Baroque and early Classical usages of the Neapolitan sixth are generally restricted to the minor key.

2. In the Baroque and Classical periods, the chord is usually employed in first inversion.
3. The sonority is derived from a *major* triad built on the *lowered second degree* of the scale; therefore II, with a probable subdominant function.
4. The chord third is normally doubled in four-voice texture.
5. The resolution is typically to V, V^7, or i_4^6.
6. The figured bass symbols are ♭6, or ♮6 in a sharped key.

Example 227

During the Romantic era, the Neapolitan sixth is used in a major key. The sonority may be employed in root position; occasionally, a chordal seventh is added.

Concerto grosso

One of the most important legacies of Baroque instrumental music is the concerto grosso, which developed over a hundred-year period from about 1650 to 1750. In addition to the contrasting concertino and ripieno instrumentation, the concerto grosso prominently displays the era's interest in instrumental idiom; in texture per se, including heterophony; and in the aspects of harmonic rhythm and pacing. Occasional fast movements have, for example, an exceedingly slow harmonic rhythm. The number of movements varies from three (Vivaldi) to five or more (Corelli)—depending upon the composer and the stage of development. Bach's six Brandenburg *Concertos* (1721) and Handel's *Grand Concertos*, Op. 6 (1740) are superb examples of this genre.

Instrumental suite

The instrumental suite is similarly a significant form, derived from the pairing of dance movements. Typically, the suite is in one key and each movement is essentially monothematic in binary or rounded binary form; i.e. A B or A B (A).

Although there is no set number of movements for the instrumental suite, an *allemande* (German), *courante* (running), *sarabande* (possibly from the Persian *serbend*, song), and *gigue* (jig) are commonly found. Optional additional movements include the air, bourrée, gavotte, loure, passepied, minuet, and other dances of the period. An easy memory guide to the suite order is A C S O (optional movements) G.

SUGGESTED STUDIES

1. Perform in class the Corelli *Largo* (Example 226), then discuss After the first reading:

Appropriate instruments

The meaning of *Largo*, tempo, dynamics, phrasing

After the second reading:

Articulation, ornamentation (trills)

After the third reading (concertato only):

Concertato parts as a musical form

After the fourth reading:

Structural, tonal, harmonic, and cadential analysis

2. In four parts, realize the following figured bass lines (Example 228a and b). Identify and label all augmented sixth and Neapolitan sixth chords. Provide an harmonic analysis.

3. Invent a complementary period to the aria with figured bass given in Example 229. Realize the figured bass in manner and style appropriate for performance as an accompaniment.

Example 228

a.

b.

Example 229

Purcell

4. Be able to discuss or write a short expository paper on a complete suite from any of Handel's sixteen keyboard suites or Bach's six French suites, covering the following:

Overall organization, including tempi and character

Tonal relationships

The design of each movement

Compositional techniques observed

Modern performance practice and problems

5. Make a keyboard realization and performing edition for a solo instrument from this movement by Handel (Example 230).

Example 230

Adagio, Op. 1, No. 2, George Frederick Handel (1685–1759)

21

CHORALE STYLE

MODULATION

CHORALE STYLE

The 371 chorale harmonizations of J. S. Bach offer significant insight into the harmonic and contrapuntal writing of the high Baroque. Chorale melodies were invented by Reformation and later Protestant composers, or they were borrowed from existing liturgical and popular sources. Bach's chorales, except for about ten, were harmonizations of existing melodies and were used as portions of larger choral compositions—particularly of the cantatas and passions.

Chorales are short compositions varying from about 12 to 50 measures. The phrase lengths correspond to the text, where typically six to eight syllables define the phrase. Although the chorales are essentially through-composed (principle of contiguity), one often observes a musical repetition of the first two phrases, resulting in a generalized AAB or *bar form*.

Bach's musical process is observed on several levels:

1. Tonal clarity, particularly in the initial and final phrases, with tonal variety as an internal feature
2. Bass lines of unusual strength and sense of direction
3. Varied internal arriving points (cadences), often implying a circular design
4. Harmonic variety within an ordered system with typically strong root movement progressions at points of cadence

Vor Deinen Thron Tret Ich Heimet (Example 231) is a version of the familiar *Old Hundredth*, derived from a *Pseaume* of Louis Bourgeois (1551). The four phrases of equal length are firmly anchored in D major without any real modulation. Harmonic progression stems from a sweeping bass line which approaches an instrumental character (Example 232).

161

Example 231

Vor Deinen Thron Tret Ich Heimet, J. S. Bach (1685–1750)

Be - fore Thy throne   I   now — ap - pear, O Lord, bow

down—Thy gra - cious   ear, Re - ject not   from — Thy

lov-ing— face A sin - ful wretch, who sues for— grace.

Example 232

Arrival points are varied. Psychologically, these cadences are of crucial importance in providing for direction, variety, and a valid musical experience. When played consecutively, the cadences form a logical harmonic progression (Example 233):

Example 233

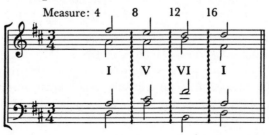

Measure: 4   8   12   16

I   V   VI   I

A comparison of progression by fifths with Bach's actual practice is of interest:

First phrase:
Progression
by fifths } I III VI II(IV) V I VI II V I

Bach's
harmonization } I VI III IV – I VI II V I

Last phrase:
Progression
by fifths } V I VI II V I II V I

Bach's
harmonization } V I VI – V I II V I

Hypothesis and practice would seem to have the greatest correlation at points of cadence. Cadences are typically strong, although in the 371 chorales there are obviously numerous exceptions. *Vor Deinen Thron* (Example 231) is ideal for initial study:

1st phrase cadence: II^6_5 V I
2nd phrase cadence: I I_6 V
3rd phrase cadence: $\dfrac{II^6_5 \quad V\sharp \quad VI}{VI}$
4th phrase cadence: II_6 V I

Without exception in this chorale, all cadence dominant and tonic chords are in *root position*.

Example 234

O haupt voll Blut und Wunden, J. S. Bach

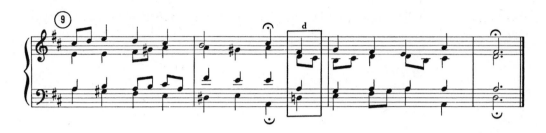

Hassler's melody of 1601, set by Bach in *O Haupt voll Blut und Wunden* (Example 234), suggests the phrygian mode and may account for the rather unusual final cadence, with a chord third in the soprano voice. The harmonization by Bach is, of course, in D major—with modulations to b minor, e minor, and A major.

MODULATION   It is recalled that there are three principal categories of modulation:
    Diatonic (common chord)
    Chromatic
    Enharmonic
Of these three, diatonic modulation is the most frequently used in the Baroque and Classical periods.
    An illustration of common sonorities of the four tonal levels of this chorale is found in Example 235:

Example 235

Well into the nineteenth century, most composers were content to utilize key relationships which were closely related to the principal key—that is, to one or two sharps or flats on either side of the tonic, as shown in Example 235. It should be observed that, although C and C♯ are immediately adjacent in terms of sound, their key relationship is seven degrees removed.

Modulatory procedure

The boxed chords in Example 234 are points of modulation and, for the purpose of emphasis, are shown below in Example 236:

Example 236

a. D V $\boxed{\begin{array}{l}\text{I} =\\ \text{III}\end{array}}$ VII$_6$ i
   b

b. b $\boxed{\begin{array}{l}\text{I} =\\ \text{VI}\end{array}}$ VII$_6$(II)   I$_6$
   D

c. D $\boxed{\begin{array}{l}\text{IV} =\\ \text{III}\end{array}}$ VII^7 I^9
   e

d. A $\boxed{\begin{array}{l}\text{IV} =\\ \text{I}\end{array}}$ II   (VII$_6$)   I$_6$
   D

In Example 234, X (measure 8) marks a chromatic area. The dominant of e minor is an altered supertonic in the key of A major; the anticipated e minor chord becomes, rather, e^{i}g$\sharp$b and d^{ii}. Chromatic modulation requires the alteration of one or more tones in the direction of the new key. In the above example, the note d^{ii} was changed from sharp to natural to affirm the tonality of A major.

Enharmonic modulation may be basically either diatonic or chromatic, but involves a respelling of chord tones in the direction of the new key (Example 237).

Example 237

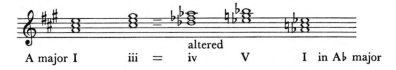

A major I   iii   =   altered iv   V   I in A♭ major

In diatonic modulation (Example 236), a common chord—called the *pivot* chord—has a function other than dominant in the new key (i.e., III, VI, or I). Avoidance of the new dominant as the pivot chord does perhaps achieve a more immediate functional clarity for the new phrase. Exceptions are found, however, especially the formula observed in Example 238e. Additional modulatory schemes are included below:

Example 238

Du Friedefürst, Herr Jesu Christ (Example 239) is quoted with two
analytical versions—a chordal analysis (I) and a structural harmonic
analysis (II) derived from the theoretical contributions of Heinrich
Schenker (1869–1935). The ability to perceive the basic harmonic
structure of a composition is a most relevant skill for the performer,
composer, and music historian. However, it should be understood
that any analytical system will contain aspects susceptible to subjective application and that any composition, irrespective of style,
fortunately may be viewed from several perspectives.

Schenker refers to the following levels of harmonic activity:

Foreground: actual progression; treble line is called *Urlinie*

Middle ground: an intervening functional level (first phase of reduction)

Background: the harmonic structure at its most basic level (*Ursatz*)

**Analytical
systems**

Example 239

Du Friedefürst, Herr Jesu Christ, J. S. Bach

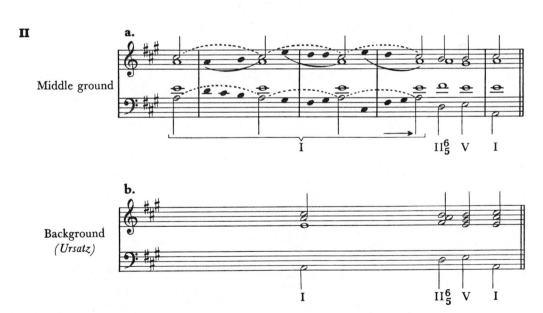

Analysis of first two phrases from *Structural Hearing* by Felix Salzer, Dover Publications, Inc., New York, 1952, Vol. II, p. 49. Reprinted through permission of the publisher.

(The author of this text refers to these levels of activity as "harmonic dimensions" and uses "substructure" synonymously with Schenker's "background.")

It is possible that analyses I and II may both omit important considerations. Analysis I perhaps appears simply as a series of related chords; Analysis II examines the harmonic resultants of linear activity at structurally significant points.

An additional analysis (III) suggests that the first four measures are concerned with an alternation of tonic and subdominant, while the final four bars balance the tonal axis with an emphasis on dominant and submediant.

Example 240

III

(♯)

In summary:

First dimension: I   IV   VII°₆   I   etc.
Second dimension: I   IV   (I)   V   VI   II°⁶₅   V   I
Third dimension   I   V   I
(substructure):

Nun Danket Alle Gott, the familiar hymn of Thanksgiving (Example 241), is analyzed in terms of non-harmonicism. The chorale is typical of Bach's usage:

13 PT   =   passing tone
3 S   =   suspension
2 ET   =   escape tone (échappée)
2 OR   =   ornamental resolution
1 NT   =   neighboring tone (auxiliary tone)
1 APT   =   accented passing tone (appoggiatura)
1 A   =   anticipation

Observations:

1. Harmonic connection of triads and seventh chords becomes an art with the assistance of judiciously used non-harmonic tones. The procedure effects a quasi-counterpoint—perhaps more implied than real—yet tension and release and rhythmic flow are accomplished essentially by embellishing and connecting tones.

Example 241

Nun Danket Alle Gott, J. S. Bach

2. Passing tones have the highest frequency of use followed, at considerable distance, by suspensions. Measures 5 and 9 contain examples of suspensions where the resolution and movement in the bass are simultaneous (Example 242a, b). In such instances the Arabic designation conforms to the actual distance between the bass and the resolving tones (Example 242).

Example 242

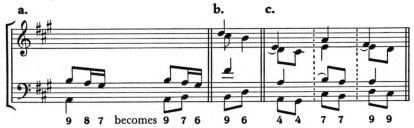

a.		b.	c.				
9 8 7 becomes 9 7 6		9 6	4 4	7 7	9 9		

Cadential decoration

The Renaissance cadential decoration is retained in Baroque practice. When involving a dissonance, the decorative figure is commonly referred to as an ornamental resolution (Example 243).

Example 243

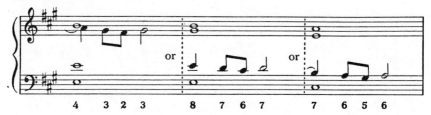

Chorale rhythm

Rhythmic flow in the chorales is regulated by the alternation of long and short, ♩ and ♪, but occasionally, especially at cadences, is intensified by common figures of shorter value: ♩. ♪ ♪, ♩ ♪ ♪, or less often ♪ ♪ ♩, and seldom ♪ ♪ ♪. Bach is typically careful to introduce in the first phrases all note values to be used subsequently in the chorale. Sudden rhythmic outbursts are not common to Bach's style, although Handel occasionally indulges in them for dramatic reasons.

Example 244

Ach Gott, Wie Manches Herzeleid, J. S. Bach

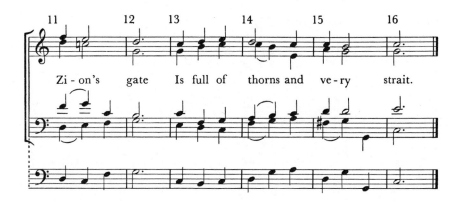

Zi - on's gate Is full of thorns and ve - ry strait.

Melodic bass,
root bass

The chorale setting of *Ach Gott, Wie Manches Herzeleid* (Example 244) illustrates again the importance of a melodic bass line—achieved in part by the employment of chord inversions for both horizontal and vertical factors. Compare Bach's actual bass with the *root bass*.

Further observations:

1. The cadence plan for the entire chorale is V/V (measure 4) V (measure 8) V (measure 12) I (measure 16), which again provides a logical progression for the arrival points.

2. Of the total 36 chords in the harmonization, observe the preponderance of dominant function:

Tonic function:	I (11)
	vi (2)
Dominant function:	V (9)
	vii° (2)
Secondary dominant function:	V/V (5)
	V/vi (2)
	V/ii (1)
Subdominant function:	IV (2)
	ii (2)
Total tonic:	13
Total dominant:	19
Total subdominant:	4

Chord disposition
(spacing)

3. Although the harmonization contains only nine different sonorities, variety is achieved by the emphasis on (or in) the dominant in the second phrase; by the use of inversions; by the addition of chordal sevenths; and by chordal disposition (i.e., the specific arrangement of pitches for a given sonority). In this simple and direct chorale, Bach tenders considerable interest in the sonorous possibilities of the tonic chord (Example 245).

Example 245

The unusual disposition (spacing) of chords in measures 13–14 probably results from linear considerations; this compositional procedure provides for still another aspect of variety.

Example 246

Es Ist Genug, J. S. Bach

Es Ist Genug (Example 246) is a chorale of singular beauty with considerable harmonic complexity. The analysis provided in Example 246 represents *one* perspective and should not be regarded as the only possible analysis. Particularly, measures 10 and 11 might well be analyzed at the level of E.

Harmonic area (region)

The chordal analyses contained within brackets are points of unusual interest, representing an harmonic activity at a level other than the central tonic. The bracket extending from measure 1 to measure 3 could be considered an *area* or *region* (mediant, in this instance) of harmonic function. Observe that in this chorale setting, the dominant region (V) has the greatest emphasis, balanced by the mediant region in the beginning and the submediant region near the end. The substructure (background or *Ursatz*) for the entire chorale could probably be defined as: I V I.

Further observations:

1. The chorale melody has strong lydian mode vestiges and the opening whole-tone movement is extraordinary. Melodic repetition is the primary principle of organization: compare measure 5 to measures 1 and 2; measures $6\frac{1}{2}$–11 to 1–$6\frac{1}{2}$; 15–17 to 12–14; 20 to 18.

2. The inner force—or perhaps "propulsion"—comes from the nearly constant alternation of tension and repose:

   Tension: measure 1–2 (chromaticism and sonorities foreign to the central tonic; fast harmonic rhythm)

 Repose: measure 3-4 (diatonic; slow harmonic rhythm; weak cadence)

3. Cadence emphasis is on I and V—which act as "anchors" in a shifting harmonic scheme (observe the chromatic bass line in measures 15-16).

4. Tone painting is of a high order, achieved not only by the poignancy of vertical tone structures but also by the non-symmetrical phrase structure and deliberately imbalanced inner accents.

1. Harmonize the following chorale melodies in four parts. Analyze the melody, considering shape of line, possible modulation implications, cadence points, melodic rhythm, harmonic rhythm.

 Sketch a bass line that will provide a melodic fluency and logical eighteenth-century harmonic progressions.

 Add the inner voices.

 Refine the harmonization by the careful addition of non-harmonic tones, appropriate to the style.

 Add an harmonic analysis.

 After completion, play the harmonizations several times.

Example 247

d.

2. Make a thorough analysis of *Wir Singen Dir, Immanuel* (Example 248), including the following:

> Harmonic and structural analyses; the role and function of non-harmonic tones
> The nature and purpose of the instrumental interludes
> Cadence plan
> Possible figured bass realizations

Example 248

Wir Singen Dir, Immanuel, Christmas Oratorio, J. S. Bach

22

HARMONIC COUNTERPOINT

CANON

SPECIES COUNTERPOINT

FUGUE

In the previous discussions of the chorales, functional harmonic progressions were shown to have partial contrapuntal implications as the result of careful control of each contributing line. Similarly, compositions which were conceived linearly (e.g. canons, fugues) are rarely observed to be without a strong harmonic basis.

CANON The concept of a circle of fifths within a key to control progression (III, VI, II, V, I) might well be expanded to embrace a rotating or circular composition such as the Kirnberger *Canon* (Example 249), which modulates through all twelve major keys. In this composition, the five-measure subject modulates from its tonic to its dominant; concurrently, each subject entry is at the perfect fifth above the preceding entry; further, after a measure and a half rest, each voice reenters at a major third above its starting note, eventually returning to the original note (an octave higher) and to the original key.

One may become fascinated primarily by the contrapuntal and modulatory aspects of this short composition; however, Kirnberger has built the work on a solid harmonic basis. Analysis of measures 1–5 illustrates:

1. C: I   (ii   vi)

2. V_6 —   vi   I

3. V_2^4 of V   vii   I   iii

4. $vi^7 =$
    G: ii^7 V^7 I   iii

5. $vi^7 =$
    D: ii^7 V^7 I   iii

178

Example 249

Canon modulating through all twelve major keys, Johann Philipp
Kirnberger (1721–1783)

Quoted in Imogene Horsley, *Fugue: History and Practice* (New York: Free Press, 1966),
pp. 28–29. Used by permission.

It is recommended that the entire composition be analyzed harmonically, with particular attention to the points of *enharmonic change*. Copying (or transposing up a half-step) will provide further insights.

**SPECIES
COUNTERPOINT
(Ricercar)**

Bach's *Ricercar* (quoted in part in Example 250) not only describes a contrapuntal procedure—producing a tonal design in the process—but its title is an example of an acronym as well. *Regis Iussu Cantio* etc. spells out "RICERCAR."[1] The *Musical Offering* contains a multitude of polyphonic devices, yet its art lies in the music it produces. (See Chapters 7 and 8, which introduce certain terminology and concepts relating to contrapuntal procedures.)

Example 250

Ricercar a 3, J. S. Bach (1685–1750)

---

[1] "By command of the King, the theme and other things developed in canonical art."

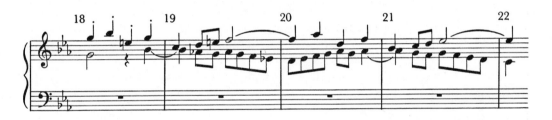

Observations:

1. The *Ricercar* begins with a nine-measure single melodic line which
   divides into three main parts:
   Measures 1–3: outline of tonic chord, producing i to vii;
   Measures 4–7: chromatically "filling in" the acquitted diminished
           7th;
   Measures 8–9: suggesting a cadence, i$^6_4$ V i. The remaining three
           beats of measure 9 form a link to the next section.
2. Measures 10–18 produce the same material as the preceding
   measures, except that the pitches are transposed down a perfect
   fourth. To this transposed material, a new line of counterpoint
   is added.
3. By judicious rhythmic control, shorter note values are gradually
   introduced which produce motion, direction, and impetus.
4. Rather than being described in the usual terms of tension and
   relaxation, Bach's passage may be described as an alternation

between clarity and ambiguity: the harmonic preciseness of the first three measures is followed by less clear harmonic implications (measures 4–7) and, in conclusion, by a clearly defined cadence. Measures 10–18 have a similar alternation.

FUGUE

Composers in the late Baroque produced few examples of the ricercar (such as the one above) and instead turned their attention to a procedure called *fugue*. The most famous collection of fugues is, of course, that of J. S. Bach's 48 preludes and fugues entitled *Das Wohltemperierte Klavier*, which may be correctly translated as: *The Well-tempered Clavier* (i.e., "keyboard").

**Terminology of
fugal analysis**

Certain terminology is commonly used in fugal analysis:

Exposition is the initial portion of a fugue, in which all voices have an opportunity of presenting the main melodic idea, called:
  Subject (*dux, leader*): the designation for a pitch group or "theme"; and
  Answer (*comes, follower*): the term which denotes that the subject has been transposed, typically to the level of the dominant. A *real answer* is an exact transposition, interval by interval;
  A *tonal answer* adjusts certain notes (particularly the melodic perfect fifth) in order to remain in the principal tonality;
  Modified real answers or *modified tonal answers* are best described collectively as *hybrid*.

Entry group describes subsequent entries of the subject (after the exposition).

Episode is the term which describes the free or developmental portions of a fugue. An episode typically does *not* contain a full statement of the subject; rather, a part of the subject is used in fragmentation, sequence, or other developmental guise.

Close and *coda* describe the final portions of the fugue.

Stretto (It., narrow, close, tight) is a term which denotes an overlapping technique (i.e., a second entry of the subject or answer prior to the completion of the first entry). Fugues in which this device is employed prominently are often referred to as *stretto fugues*.

Voice refers to the number of contrapuntal lines employed in any given composition. The *WTC* contains fugues from two-voice texture (a 2) to five-voice textures (a 5), with three- and four-voice fugues being the most numerous.

Two fugues from the *WTC*, Volume I, are quoted in their entirety for the purpose of showing two architectural types.

Example 251

Fuga I, WTC, Volume I, J. S. Bach

Example 252

Fuga II, WTC, Volume I, J. S. Bach

Subject-structured fugue

Fuga I (Example 251) is a *subject-structured* fugue. Other terminologies, such as "subject-centered" and "subject-oriented," are synonymous.

Observations:

1. The subject (in brackets) is one and one-half measures long; it is answered at the perfect fifth above (real answer), continues with another answer (which is unusual) at the perfect fourth below the original subject, and concludes the exposition with the subject an octave below the original.
2. Thereafter, the contrapuntal procedure is such that the subject (or answer) is presented in all measures except 23 and 26-27. Hence the term: *subject-structured.*
3. In lieu of episodes, *Fuga I* contains two stretto sections—becoming increasingly complex in the number of simultaneous presentations of the subject.
4. Finally, in measure 24, the subject appears again in the tonic (and subdominant), indicating the conclusion or *close* of the composition.

A structural diagram of *Fuga I* would be as follows:

Measures:	1–6	7–13		14–22		23	24–27
Description or function:	exposition	stretto	1	stretto 2		LINK	close
Tonality:	C	G	a	a D G C			C

Sophisticated in vocabulary and structure, *Fuga I* entices a kind of speculative theory, or the discovering of relationships and associations which penetrate beyond the purely surface features. A few additional observations may suggest further analysis:

1. The circled notes of measures 1 and 2 seem to define important aspects of the whole fugue:
   a. The basic tonal plan of the entire fugue: C G a (D) G C.
   b. The basic harmonic progression which, at different rhythmic rates, seems to pervade much of the fugue: I   V   vi   ii   V   I
   (II♯)
2. The note f^i in measure 1 displays its structural importance in measures 5-6, and again in measures 24-26.

Episode-structured fugue

Fuga II (Example 252) differs substantially from *Fuga I* in the character of the subject and, assuredly, in its structuring. *Fuga II* is an example of an *episode-structured* fugue.

Observations:

1. The subject of measures 1-2 is answered tonally at the perfect

fifth above. It is observed that the original interval of a perfect fourth is now modified to a perfect fifth.

2. Prior to the entry of the subject in the bass, a two-bar *episode* is inserted (measures 5–6). These bars contain a sequential treatment of the opening motive. The restatement of the subject in measures 7–8 brings the exposition to a close.

3. Thereafter, the structuring of *Fuga II* consists of an alternation of "strict" and "free" presentations, as shown in the accompanying table:

Measures:	1–2	3–4	5–6	7–8
Description/ function:	Subject	Answer	Free sequence	Subject
Structure:	Exposition		Episode 1*	Completion of exposition
Tonality	c	c to g	g to c	c

*This first episode might be considered as a structural link.

9–10	11–12	13–14	15–16	17–19
Free sequence	Subject "strict"	Free sequence	Subject	Free, but inversion of measure 5
Episode 2	Entry group II	Episode 3	Entry group III	Episode 4
c to E♭	E♭	E♭	g	g to c

20–21	22–middle of 26	26 (beat 3)– 29 (beat 3)	29–31
Subject	Expansion of material from measure 9	Subject (close)	Subject coda
Entry group IV	Episode 5	Entry group V	
c	E♭, c	c	c

Further observations:

1. Hence, the basic tonal plan is: c (g) c E♭ g c (E♭) c. Those areas marked () are non-structural tonal areas, but are nevertheless interesting in terms of balance and symmetry.

2. With the exception of the coda, each subject entry is accompanied by a consistent and persistent musical idea, marked ~~~~~~~~~~~~~~.
   This accompanying counterpoint is referred to as a *counter-subject*.

3. An additional counterpoint, initially observed in measure 8 (marked X——X——X——X) may be considered either as a second counter-subject or possibly as a contrapuntal associate. Although its appearance is persistent throughout the remainder of the composition, its musical role seems subservient to the subject and principal counter-subject.

4. The gradual lengthening of the episodes from two measures to three measures (17–19), to four and one-half measures (22–26), provides for asymmetry and non-predictability of structure. In fact, it might be argued that Bach really effected a metrical change in measure 22—where the third beat might become the first beat of a new measure.

5. Bach provides for variety of color and register by his judicious control of each entry of the subject.

Example 253

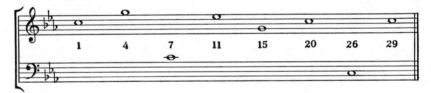

Per item 4 above, observe the expanding arithmetical series.

6. Once again the subtleties of Bach's technique, which are revealed with each successive analysis, are nearly inexhaustible.

SUGGESTED STUDIES

1. Be prepared to discuss Baroque melodic types, contours, harmonic outlines from the examples presented in the text.

2. Write a short modulatory or circular canon with the Kirnberger *Canon* (Example 249) as a model.

3. Write the *exposition* of a fugue a 3, using *Fuga II* (Example 252) as a model.

4. Write a short expository paper on the development of fugue from c. 1600 to 1750.

5. Study and be able to sing any of the fugue subjects from the *WTC*.

6. Compare J. S. Bach's fugues with that of Johann Fischer (c. 1665–1746) quoted below in Example 254.

Example 254

From *Ariadne Musica*, Fugue, Johann Kaspar Ferdinand Fischer
(c. 1665–1746)

23

STRUCTURAL HARMONY

CLASSICAL DESIGN

SONATA PRINCIPLE

CANON CANCRIZANS

STRUCTURAL HARMONY

Rhythm, melody, texture, color, and harmony are usually significant only in a syntactical framework. Depending upon the emphasis designed by the composer, these elements either define or contribute to the organic whole. The study of melodic and harmonic *rhythm* may reveal the composer's pacing of musical events; *melody* may suggest the composer's attitudes towards expression and meaning of music; *texture* and *color* may suggest the musical environment; finally *harmony* (obviously in compositions where this element is a contributing parameter) may provide important clues regarding musical architecture. Structural harmony refers to groups of sonorities or chords. Such a group, by reasons of function or interrelation, may define phrase or periodicity. Larger harmonic groupings may confirm tonality as well as a basic structure. One studies the parts (harmony) in order to comprehend the whole (structure and form).

In the time-space continuum, a single pitch (already a "chord" by virtue of its overtones) may be viewed in several of its horizontal dimensions. By way of illustration, consider a single tone in its relationship to a three-movement sonata:

	1 second	12 seconds	2 minutes	15 minutes
pitch (chord)	progression	cadence	tonal orientation	structure

The internal relationships of *chord-tonality-structure* were perhaps in their most perfect agreement during the Classical era, approximately 1760 to 1810.

Example 255

Sonata No. 1, Franz Joseph Haydn (1732–1809)

**CLASSICAL
DESIGN**

Example 255 quotes in its entirety the *Piano Sonata* No. 1[1] by Franz Joseph Haydn (1732–1809). *Sonata* (It. *suonare*, to sound) is the term frequently applied to compositions (typically for one or two performers) in which structural organization and unity are of prime importance. Obviously, trios, quartets, quintets, symphonies are "sonatas" for varying instrumental combinations. Although there exist keyboard sonatas of one movement (Scarlatti) and five movements (Brahms), two- to four-movement works are more common. During the late eighteenth century, the three-movement, fast-slow-fast sonata became the norm. The internal design of each movement was primarily limited to the following:

Binary
Ternary
Rondo
Theme and variations
Menuet (typically with trio)
Sonata-allegro

Nearly without exception, "form" resides in, and results from, the careful control of tonal organization in all the above categories. A given movement may be made up of themes or of motives; it may involve strongly contrasting ideas or, conversely, may be *mono-thematic*. Although proportions, repetitions, and the spacing of events are obviously important considerations in any musical design, the most constant and predictable factor in relation to Classical forms would seem to be the tonal organization of each movement and of the composition as a whole.

The brief digest of Classical forms listed below is intended as a general guide for initial studies.

Binary (bi-partite principle):

A			B			Repeats and repetitions vary from
I	to	V	V	to	I	movement to movement.
i	to	III	III	to	i	V (or III in a minor key) may be actual tonal levels or simply a chordal emphasis. There are exceptions, of course, to the I to V (III) schemata.

Balanced proportions are important for the bi-partite principle, although an expanded B-section is very common. (For a simple binary form see Example 255, *Andante*.)

Ternary (tri-partite principle):

A		B		A	or	A		BA	or	Aa	Bb	Aa˙
I		to	V to	I		etc.						

[1] Early Haydn sonatas bore diverse titles such as *Divertimento* or *Partita*. These compositions are now included, however, in the complete *Sonatas*. (See Vienna Urtext Edition, 1965.)

Typically the B-section emphasizes a chord or tonal center other than the tonic.

Rondo (principle of return):

A B A B A   Small (or second) Rondo
         C

A B A C A B A   Large (or third) Rondo

In both versions of the rondo, thematic and tonal digressions are consistently observed. The B-sections are typically in the dominant or mediant tonality; C-sections provide for further tonal digression—often to the subdominant, submediant, or to the parallel mode. Haydn frequently employed the principle of variation for his returning or repeated sections, thus fusing form and procedure.[2]

Variation:

The most frequently observed technique of variation in the Classical period is that of thematic elaboration within a set structural and harmonic framework. The "theme" and its initial harmonization usually define a simple binary or simple ternary design. This set structure is then typically maintained for each variation; similarly, the basic harmonic progression supporting the theme is commonly retained (with or without disguise) throughout the entire movement—or independent composition.

Menuet and trio:

The menuet (typically with trio) is one of the durable designs of the Classical era. The term *menuet* describes a dance and possibly suggests the character and tempo of the composition. Depending on the temperament of the composer, the terms *song* or *scherzo* (see Mendelssohn and Beethoven) are substituted. The basic structure remains the same, however. The most typical appearance is as shown below:

Menuet	*Trio*	*Menuet*	
A:‖ BA:‖	C:‖ DC:‖	ABA	(most often indicated *Da capo* after the Trio section). (in the return, internal repeat signs are not observed).

The B-sections typically achieve a tonal variety; similarly, the trio rarely remains in the same key or mode as the menuet. The design as a whole, of course, forms a *compound ternary*. Compare Haydn's *Menuet* (Example 255) to the above structural plan.

---

[2] There are surprisingly few examples of *Rondo* or *Theme and Variations* in the piano sonatas of Haydn and Mozart.

SONATA PRINCIPLE

Sonata-allegro

By far the most widely employed structure of the Classical era—in sonatas, quartets, concertos, and symphonies—is the so-called *sonata-allegro*, also, unfortunately, referred to as the *first-movement form*. Of all the names assigned to Classical forms, sonata-allegro (to sound, cheerfully) or first-movement form are the most misleading, inadequate, and initially confusing. This design, the *sonata principle*, appears in all moods and tempos; it serves as a first, middle, or last movement; it has a few or many themes; and, despite these seeming ambiguities, is basically the most vibrant, flexible, and energizing organizational premise to emerge from the Classical era. Early appearances of this organizational premise (mid-eighteenth century) bear a close resemblance to the binary form of the Baroque era; thereafter, its most distinguishing feature is that of a clearly delineated middle section, termed "development," thus changing the proportions to ternary. A brief outline of the sonata principle follows:

EXPOSITION	DEVELOPMENT	RECAPITULATION
Statement of ideas	Elaboration of ideas	Restatement and summation of ideas
Duality of tonalties (I to V is typical)	Multiplicity of tonalities	Unity of tonality emphasis on I
Group I (first tonal area) *transition* or connective link; typically modulates. Group II (second tonal area) Repeat of exposition.	Development sections vary from movement to movement. With some frequency one observes several key areas related by fifths and a clear preparation (by dominant pedal) for the return of the opening material.	In the recapitulation, it is typical that Group I and Group II remain in the tonic key. Indications for repetition of the development and recapitulation vary.

None of the Haydn or Mozart keyboard sonatas have a slow *introduction*, as is the case in some symphonies; a few sonatas do have a final summation, however, which is referred to as a *coda*. *Hybrid forms* are beyond the discussions of this text. The crossing of sonata and rondo principles, the menuet with variation techniques, etc., are occasionally observed.

The musical structure described above inherently provides for unity and diversity, predictability and surprise, event and the connection of events. Pacing as well as dramatic shape are the physiological and the psychological factors involved in the successful rendering of the sonata form—or preferably, the sonata principle.

Haydn's *Sonata No. 1* is a model of simplicity. The first movement employs, perhaps in its embryonic stage, the sonata principle—satisfying the tonal requirements in the exposition and again in the recapitulation. The equivalent of the development section functions as a free fantasy and connection to the return. The *Menuet* movement, without *Trio*, is a simple binary; the same structural principles are used in the *Andante* movement. Haydn's final *Allegro* is a simple ternary, with sufficient digression (B) to provide interest for the repetition of A.

The harmonic vocabulary is as straightforward as the structure, with primary triads providing the basis of the harmonic language. Further, selected chords define both phrase and periodicity; finally, structure emerges from harmonic manipulation. A Baroque feature is

Example 256

The Ten Commandments, Franz Joseph Haydn

3 parts
Canon cancrizans (Crab canon)*

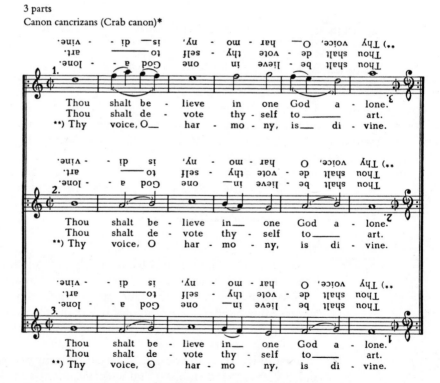

*This canon can be sung forwards or backwards, either right side up or upside down.
**Haydn's text on receiving an honorary doctorate from Oxford University.

retained: all movements are in the same key. Most other sonatas, however, have a tonally contrasting middle movement.

Haydn's melodies are direct and almost as simple as folk songs. Short rhythmic cells or motives engage in a free exchange and stimulate a most interesting dimension.

CANON CANCRIZANS (Crab canon)

A simple chordal progression is typically observed as the basis of contrapuntal writing during the Classical era. Such is the case with Haydn's *serio-buffo* opus entitled *The Ten Commandments* (Example 256). As Haydn and the editors advise, the canon can be sung forwards or backwards, right side up or upside down. Further, from these modest six measures, a total of 206 bars of music can be projected if all verses and versions are sung.

SUGGESTED STUDIES

1. Write a short expository paper on the emergence of the sonata principle in the eighteenth century.
2. Make a Schenker-type analysis for each of the movements in Example 255.
3. Compose a crab canon, using Haydn's first *Commandment* as a model (Example 256).
4. Compose a Trio for the *Menuet* movement of Haydn's Sonata No. 1 (Example 255) in an appropriate keyboard style. Use a contrasting key.
5. Make an harmonic, melodic, and structural analysis of the following *Trio* (Example 257). Comment also on appropriate tempo, dynamics, control of texture, contrapuntal interplay, compositional devices employed.

Example 257

Trio, Op. 64, No. 5, Franz Joseph Haydn

24

NINTH CHORDS
DIMINISHED SEVENTHS
THIRD RELATIONSHIPS
ANALYTICAL PROBLEMS
CHORDAL MUTATION

NINTH CHORDS The harmonic vocabularies of the principal composers of the Classical era—including Haydn, Mozart, and Beethoven—were primarily confined to triadic and seventh-chord structures, secondary functions, and occasional altered chords such as the augmented sixth, Neapolitan sixth, and diverse seventh chords involving one or more alterations. Each of the above-named composers became quite experimental, however, in his mature and late works, and jointly they contributed to new concepts in harmonic language, chordal and tonal relationships, and general musical syntax.

Ninth chords may be observed in Baroque compositions—but mainly as contrapuntal coincidences involving *appoggiature* or other non-harmonic tones; most of these appearances seem to suggest a lack of independence as an individual chord. The principal exception would be the vii°7, functioning as an *incomplete dominant ninth*. This chord is incomplete in the sense that the root of the chord is absent. Implied by Rameau's theory and affirmed by distinguished theorists since that time, the question of *implied* roots prompts serious and provocative discussion of a composer's intent. Example 258 briefly illustrates:

Example 258

c minor: vii°7   implied root: G

The *complete* ninth chord was used with considerable frequency in the nineteenth century. As a *dominant* ninth the sonority achieved a special vogue, although its appearances were certainly not limited exclusively to dominant function. Succinctly—to any triad, or triad with seventh, a chordal ninth may be added (Example 259):

Example 259

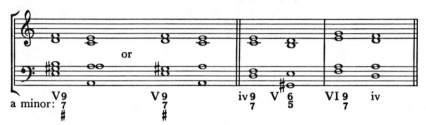

In most instances of ninth-chord usage, the chordal seventh also appears, and typically both the ninth and the seventh resolve step-wise down. In a four-voice texture, the chord fifth is omitted.

**DIMINISHED
SEVENTHS**

The *diminished seventh chord*, with at least two names—diminished-diminished, or doubly diminished—is also observed in Baroque music, but its widest adoption came during the Romantic era. The diminished-diminished seventh is poignant in sonority; it fits the keyboardist's hand remarkably well; and it holds a special theoretical fascination because of its makeup of equidistant minor thirds, its *aural* non-invertibility, and its great flexibility in resolution. Further, the basic sonority is capable of only *two* transpositions—thereafter, duplication takes place. Example 260 illustrates:

Example 260

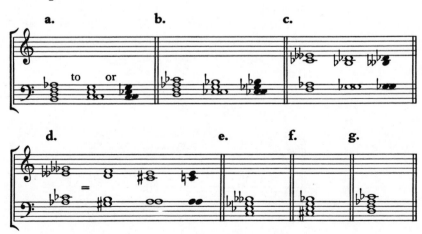

a. Basic chord in C major or c minor
b. Same sonority, using original chord third as new root
c. Same sonority, using original chord fifth as new root
d. Same sonority, using original chord seventh as new root
e. Basic chord transposed up a half-step
f. Basic chord transposed up a whole-step
g. Observe that chord *g* is a duplication of chord *b*.

As indicated above, the diminished-diminished seventh may resolve to either a major or a minor triad, which effects eight possible resolutions for each of the basic forms of the chord. Further, the half-step alteration of any *one* chord member will result in a dominant seventh (Mm) formation (Example 261):

Example 261

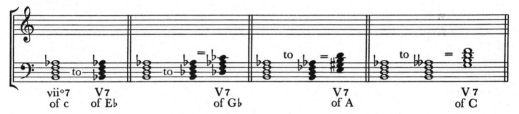

Finally, as a negotiator for quick modulations, the diminished-diminished seventh is without peer in the tertian vocabulary. From C major to eb minor or from c minor to f# minor, each of which are six degrees removed, the processes are simple—even if sometimes blatant (Example 262):

Example 262

An excerpt from Schubert's *Du bist die Ruh'* (Example 263) shows a non-modulatory use of the diminished-diminished seventh sonority (measure 41). The same song contains an excellent example of a subtle change of mode. As will be recalled, the terminology for this process is *interchangeability of modes* or *bi-modality* (see measures 55–57).

Example 263

From *Du bist die Ruh'*, Franz Schubert (1797–1828)

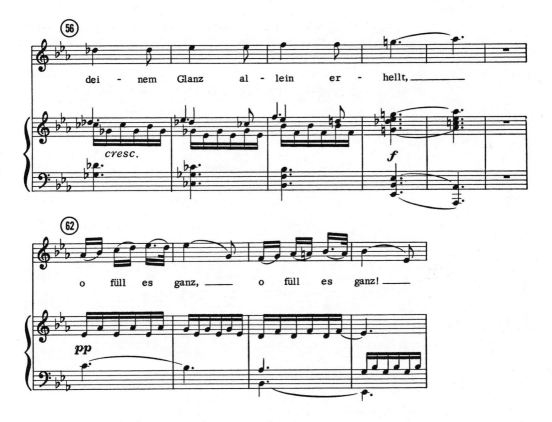

dei - nem Glanz al - lein er - hellt,_____

o füll es ganz, _____ o füll es ganz! _____

THIRD
RELATIONSHIPS

Bi-modal third relationships are observed as early as the sixteenth century. Sometimes presenting multiple cross-relations, the pungency and freshness of sound obviously fascinated many generations of composers.

Example 264

No. 92, Cosimo Bottegari (1554–1620)

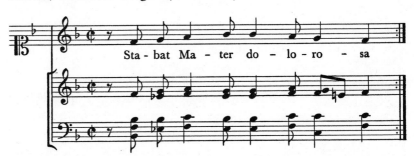

Sta - bat Ma - ter do - lo - ro - sa

From *The Bottegari Lutebook* (Wellesley Edition No. 8, 1965), ed. Carol MacClintock. Used by permission.

Ju - xta cru - cem la - cri - mo - - sa,

From the late eighteenth century through the late nineteenth century, harmonic and tonal relationship by third held a special interest for composers. Additional examples will serve to illustrate:

Example 265

As in Haydn

root becomes
Chord third

D major: V   I   Bb major: I   V   I6

Example 266

As in Robert Schumann

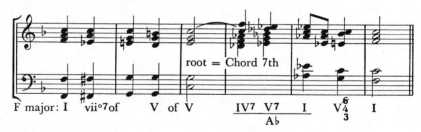

root = Chord 7th

F major: I   vii°7of   V of V   IV7 V7   I   V$\frac{6}{4}$ I
                                              Ab   3

**ANALYTICAL
PROBLEMS**

Enharmonicism

As previously explained, *enharmonic modulation* involves a respelling from sharps to flats, or the reverse. When confronted by analytical problems which include enharmonicism, the visual aspect of the page can often supply important clues. Examples 267 below serves as a case in point.

Observations:

1. The key of the entire sonata (*Pathétique*) is c minor; the principal tonality of the *Adagio* movement is Ab major (i.e., a relationship of a major third).
2. At the juncture shown above (measures 41–44), the mode has

Example 267

Excerpt from *Piano Sonata*, Op. 13, second movement *Adagio*, Ludwig van Beethoven (1770–1827)

changed to a♭ minor and, as notated, a modulation has been made to E major.

3. Therefore, as notated, an a♭ minor triad (measure 44) is enharmonically a g♯ minor triad: old key i equals new key iii.
4. Further, one should consider two somewhat contradictory views of the tonality of this passage:
   a. In relationship to c minor, E major is the bi-modal third above.
   b. In relationship to A♭, not E but rather F♭ is the bi-modal third below.

   Obviously, notation in E is easier to read than in the theoretical key of F♭ (eight flats).

An additional example of enharmonic change is shown in Hugo Wolf's song, *Das Verlassene Maegdlein,* measures 17–21.

Example 268

Measures 17–21, *Das Verlassene Maegdlein,* Hugo Wolf (1860–1903)

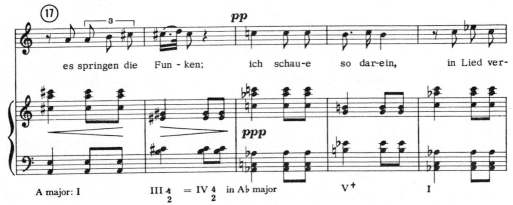

Chromaticism

Throughout the nineteenth century, composers felt free to alter any or all chord members of a given tertian structure according to their compositional needs and dictates. Pronounced or continuous chordal alteration resulted in *chromaticism*. Chromaticism, together with frequent modulations and an abundance of non-harmonicism, initially effected an expansion of the tertian system; the overuse of the procedures late in the century forewarned of the decline and near collapse of the system.

Altered chords

It is certainly not necessary to identify the profusion of altered chords employed throughout the nineteenth century. Altered chords are typically easy to distinguish in analysis and, similarly, easy to imitate in writing. A few alterations do, however, merit special consideration. Example 269 demonstrates several common formations.

Example 269

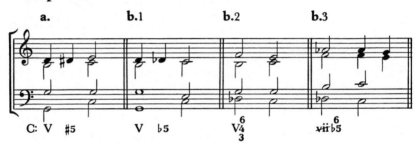

a. Raised fifth of the chord.

b1. Flatted fifth of the chord.

b2. The same sonority as b1 becomes a *dominant* augmented sixth chord when inverted.

b3. Similarly, an augmented sixth chord may be built from the *leading tone triad*.

c1. Raised root of the chord.

c2. c1, when inverted, again produces an augmented sixth chord.

c3. c1 may be (and in practice often is) respelled as a *doubly augmented sixth* chord.

It is generally true that an alteration of the chord third does not change the function of the chord. Observe the alterations in Example 270.

Example 270

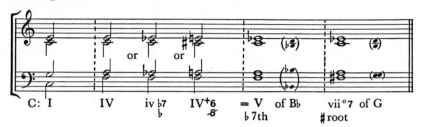

An excerpt from *Ich will meine Seele tauchen* by Robert Schumann (Example 271) illustrates actual usage of altered chords in the first part of the nineteenth century.

Example 271

From *Ich will meine Seele tauchen*, Robert Schumann (1810–1856)

Observations:

1. Alteration of iv^7 to include the flatted fifth (measure 13).
2. A chain of major–major seventh chords (measures 13–14) adds diatonic interest.
3. The subdominant "region" is explored in measures 17–18.
4. The mediant triad III$^6_3$ functions as a passing dominant (measure 19)—or simply as a melodic function between IV$_6$ and II$_6$.

One of Schumann's most eloquent and interesting *Lieder* is the opening song of his *Dichterliebe* cycle, *Im Wunderschönen Monat Mai* (Example 272). Harmonic analysis of this composition reveals an absence of the tonic chord. Tonality per se is nevertheless firmly entrenched, resulting from the non-ambiguous functioning of the dominant chord at two important cadences. The dominant seventh in the final measure serves as a preparation for the next song in the cycle.

For obvious musical reasons, Chopin's *Prelude in E Minor*, Op. 28, No. 4, is performed by most keyboard students. Yet, despite its familiarity, it is probably rarely analyzed because of the quite formidable problems it presents (Example 273).

Example 272

Im Wunderschönen Monat Mai, Robert Schumann

p (a tempo)

Im wun - der schön - en Mo-nat

Mai,   als al - le Vö - gel san -gen,   da

hab' ich ihr ge-stan - den   mein Seh - nen und - Ver-

- lan-gen.

ritard.

(attacca)

VI   (iv) V 7

Example 273

Prelude in E Minor, Op. 28, No. 4, Frédéric Chopin (1809–1849)

CHORDAL
MUTATION

The fluid and harmonically evasive left hand of Chopin's *Prelude* employs a technique common to the nineteenth century which, for lack of a better term, will be called *chordal mutation*. The term is used to describe a gradual harmonic change, or perhaps evolution, of a given starting sonority. The first five measures—as well as the remainder of the *Prelude*—illustrate this technique.

Example 274

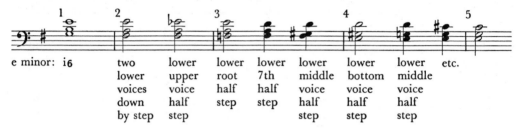

e minor: i6

| two lower voices down by step | lower upper voice half step | lower root half step | lower 7th half step | lower middle voice half step | lower bottom voice half step | lower middle voice half step | etc. |

While a modest amount of insight may be derived from a chord-by-chord analysis of the *Prelude* (Example 273), the results reveal neither the procedure nor the basic harmonic structure of the composition. Chopin eschews traditional chordal relationships and suggests perhaps a kind of non-functional harmonic movement. A Schenker-type analysis (Example 275), however, gives considerable insight into the basic structures.

Example 275

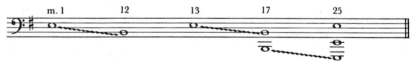

Further, a reduction of the expressive upper line of the composition (Example 276) begins to unravel Chopin's enigma.

Example 276

*Approximate durations are shown (o = 4 measures) to illustrate Chopin's control of time-span.

Observations:

1. The dramatic high point is found in measure 17—achieved by a dominant ninth which supports a flamboyant melisma; an *appoggiatura chord* further heightens the tension in this measure.

2. The basic melodic structure would appear to be derived from two descending scale fragments which together utilize all pitches from e¹ to b¹, with the exception of f♮¹.

3. Measure 23 contains a most interesting sonority. In many editions, the bass note is written as B♭ rather than A♯. In a theoretical sense, A♯ (i.e. the leading tone to V) is preferred to B♭. At least two interpretations of the chord are possible:

   a. B♭ C♮ e¹ g, a substitution for B♭ C♯ e¹ g, vii°⁷ of V;
   b. As spelled, a German augmented sixth chord in *root position*.

SUGGESTED STUDIES
1. Provide an harmonic analysis for the following excerpt. Include a short expository amplification of your analysis.

Example 277

From *Intermezzo*, Op. 116, No. 6, Johannes Brahms (1833–1897)

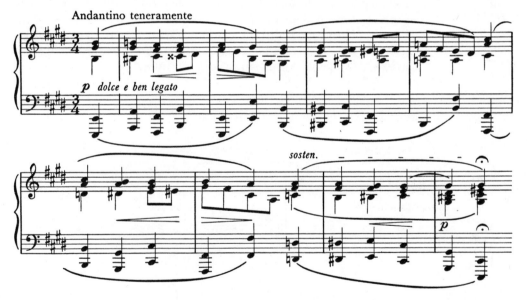

2. Write a short composition for piano using diminished–diminished seventh chords for purposes of modulation. Include one or more examples of enharmonic modulation.

3. On a text in English, write a short song (about 20 measures), using the melodic, harmonic, rhythmic vocabularies typical of Schumann or Chopin.

25

CHROMATIC ANALYSIS
HARMONIC SEQUENCE
PLURALITY OF TONAL AXES
EXTENDED APPOGGIATURA

CHROMATIC ANALYSIS

Detailed harmonic analysis of nineteenth-century compositions poses problems which demand both a critical judgement and considerable tenacity. However veiled the composer's intent may seem initially, a system is always discernible and not infrequently one finds behind the surface complexity rather simple organizational premises.

Example 278

Excerpts from *Variations Symphoniques*, César Franck (1822–1890)

The analyses which are included in this chapter offer possible solutions, to which others should be added. Subjective, at least in part, the observations are perhaps appropriate to the *Zeitgeist*, or spirit of the times, of high Romanticism.

Observations on Example 278:

1. The two excerpts illustrate parallel phrase construction: the first in f♯ minor, the second in A major-minor.
2. Chordal structures in measures 6, 7 and 14, 15 are partially resultants of the descending bass lines.
3. Chromatic evasiveness internally in the phrases is countered by cadence strength and clarity.
4. In both phrases, observe the chromatic but resolute movement from V of V to V to I.

**HARMONIC
SEQUENCE**

The harmonic structure in Example 279 is governed quite consistently by a convergence of the outside voices:

Example 279

Sleep motive from *Die Walküre*, Richard Wagner (1813–1883)

Implied bass line

Observations:

1. The upper voice descends by half-step; a two-bar rhythmic pattern effects a sequence in which the repetition occurs a major third lower for each presentation.
2. The lower voice similarly is a two-bar sequence, ascending, in which the repetition is at the minor sixth above. Observe the interval inversion of the soprano sequence; i.e., E_1 up to C; C up to G♯; G♯ up to the final e.

**PLURALITY
OF TONAL AXES**

One possible approach to the harmonic analysis of this passage is to consider a *plural* or *multiple* tonal axis; i.e., tonal axes or tonal centers which function concurrently.

G♯(A♭)————————————is the upper parallel axis
E————————————is the principal tonal axis (center)
C/c————————————is the lower parallel axis

Observe that by using the above concept of plurality of tonal axes, all chords in the excerpt function with reasonable clarity in a traditional sense.

Analysis by chord number:

1. I in E
2. V in G$\sharp$(A$\flat$); also III in c
3. x (B$\flat$ and E$\flat$ are suspensions to the next chord)
4. vii^7 in C

5. I in C
6. III in c; also V in G$\sharp$(A$\flat$)
7. V/V in C
8. I$^6_4$ (plus flatted chordal seventh); actually a mispelled vii^7 of G$\sharp$— i.e., F$^{\times}$ A$\sharp$ C$\sharp$ E

9. I in G$\sharp$
10. V in E
11. V/V in G$\sharp$(A$\flat$)
12. vii^7 in E

13. I in E

Alternate analyses to the above are encouraged. Too often analysis of chromatic music of the late Romantic period is purely descriptive, with little attention directed toward melodic and harmonic movement, and the relationships which form its basis.

Motivic construction   The fact that the musical fabric is formed from motives or, in the Wagnerian term, *leitmotifs* (G., leading or guiding motive) which represent characters, moods, aspirations, and philosophical commentary, need not deter one from technical analysis of the composer's methods of controlling the horizontal-vertical time-span. Prior to the study of a chordal analysis of the first 24 measures of the Prelude to *Tristan und Isolde* (Example 280), a few explanations are pertinent:

1. A scheme of plural tonal axes again seems to be implied:

$$A/a \underline{\quad\quad \overset{E/e}{\underset{C/c}{\quad\quad\quad\quad}} \quad\quad}\text{principal axis, both major and minor}$$

EXTENDED APPOGGIATURA
2. The *appoggiature* in this work (and many others) are lengthened to the extent that often the duration is several times longer than that of the chord tone to which they resolve (as examples, see measures 1 and 2).
3. Altered chords, especially augmented sixth chords, are coequal in importance with diatonic sonorities.
4. Harmonic and melodic sequences are abundant.
5. Cadence evasion, elision, and deception are facets of the compositional process.

Example 280

Measures 1–24, Prelude to *Tristan und Isolde*, Richard Wagner

Obviously not all passages of Wagner and Franck are as chromatic
as those cited in the previous examples. Indeed, chromaticism was
used in varying degrees by nineteenth-century composers—depending of course on individual preferences. Example 281 illustrates an

**Four-voice,
non-chromatic
texture**

Example 281

Excerpt from *Ein Deutsches Requiem*, Johannes Brahms (1833–1897)

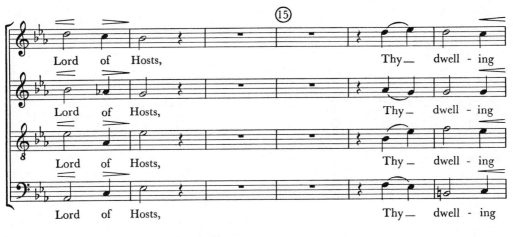

essentially non-chromatic passage from *Ein Deutsches Requiem* by
Brahms. The orchestral accompaniment is omitted.

Observations:

1. Each of the four lines is expressively contoured—suggesting a
   contrapuntal-harmonic conception.
2. The bass line has a particular independence as well as a special
   relationship to the soprano line (i.e., suggested mirror, non-strict
   imitation).
3. The overlapping phrase structure between the upper three voices
   and the basses in measures 8–9 relates to Renaissance practice.
4. The phrase structure of three bars plus five bars (measures 16–23)
   is an architectural feature of interest.
5. The stability of E♭ major and the eventual modulation to the
   dominant (via c minor) suggests a conservative view of tonal
   relationships.

Example 282

Measures 25–44, Prelude to *Tristan und Isolde*, Richard Wagner

1. Provide a motivic and harmonic analysis of measures 25–44 of the Prelude to *Tristan und Isolde* (Example 282).
2. Using primary or secondary sources, write a short expository paper on the use of the *motif* for compositional unification in nineteenth-century music. See: Berlioz, Liszt, Wagner, Franck.
3. Complete the following fragment (Example 283) to four voices as appropriate. Invent a contrasting section; repeat the beginning with slight variation.

Example 283

Adapted from Brahms

4. Complete and continue Example 284 for at least ten additional measures. Imitations, augmentations, and other polyphonic devices employed need not be strict or canonic.

Example 284

Adapted from Brahms

PART IV
The Final Expansion of the Major-Minor System; Newer Harmonic Supplements

"Mankind are very odd Creatures: One half censure what they practise, the other half practise what they censure; the rest always say and do as they ought."

—Benjamin Franklin

26

ELEVENTH, THIRTEENTH CHORDS
PARALLEL HARMONY
ADDED TONE TECHNIQUE

ELEVENTH, THIRTEENTH CHORDS

In the latter part of the nineteenth century, harmonic practice not only included chordal and melodic chromaticism, frequent modulations to distant key centers, and prolongation of non-harmonic tones, but the tertian system itself expanded to encompass sonorities beyond seventh and ninth chords. A new phase began, of increased use of non-harmonic tones which gradually became harmonic. The resulting eleventh chords, and especially thirteenth chords, were used with some frequency in the continuing search for new resources within the major-minor system. Example 285 illustrates several common formations.

Example 285

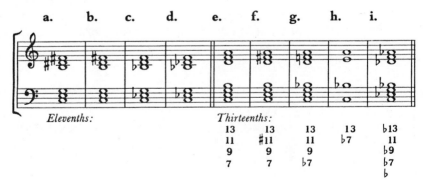

Observations:

1. The eleventh chord may be considered as an expansion beyond the ninth; or as two triads, superimposed vertically, and related

227

by an interval of a third. In Example 285a, the eleventh chord consists of a C major triad and a B major triad producing, in effect, a *polychord*.

2. Similarly, as in Example 285i, the thirteenth chord may be comprised of a seventh chord (Cmm^7) plus a triad (D♭ major).

3. Although a kind of artificial figured bass may be devised—by simply taking an inventory above the bass note—the practice is not recommended, since composers ceased using this musical shorthand about 1760.[1]

4. Perhaps the most common usage of these chords was the dominant thirteenth (Example 285g), which is a V^7 with diatonic expansion. Example 285h shows a four-voice version which includes a root, third, seventh, and thirteenth. This disposition is typical. Most often the chordal seventh will resolve step-wise down, but the thirteenth is free to
   a. remain stationary
   b. move down
   c. leap up

Example 286

Resolutions:

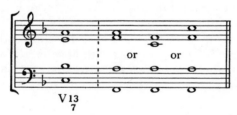

$$V\,{}^{13}_{7}$$

Of interest, as a theoretical point, is that the complete seven-voice thirteenth chord is non-invertible. Any attempt at first, second, etc., inversion simply produces a new chord with a different root.

Example 287

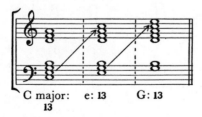

C major: e: 13   G: 13
13

---

[1] In some sacred music, however, figured bass practice continued well into the nineteenth century.

The following excerpt from Alexander Scriabine's *Prelude*,
Op. 48, No. 4 (Example 288), shows an extensive use of expanded
tertian sonorities derived from linear considerations.

Example 288

Excerpt from *Prelude*, Op. 48, No. 4, Alexander Scriabine
(1872–1915)

Observations:

1. Although most vertical sonorities include the seventh, ninth,
   eleventh, or thirteenth, the basic harmonic progressions are
   strongly anchored to the concept of root movement by fifths.
2. Two examples of root movement by tri-tone (measures 17–18,
   D♭–G and the same notes in measures 19–22) are supportive of
   a certain dissonant character of this *Prelude*.
3. The chordal dispositions covering five and a half octaves (measure
   23) further indicate the expansiveness of concept and mood.

**PARALLEL
HARMONY**

In the two decades from about 1890 to 1910, several musical cross-
currents rather radically influenced the direction of Western music.
The highly expanded tertian system, illustrated above, was modified

by numerous composers by the introduction of one or more of the
following influences:

1. Medieval and Renaissance music, and reuse of a modified modal
   system.
2. Use of folk song materials, which resulted in a certain simplifica-
   tion of the tertian system.
3. Interest in certain exotic elements such as the pentatonic scales,
   Iberian rhythms, quasi-Oriental clarity of texture, etc. In orchestral
   music these items were frequently coupled to a highly coloristic
   scoring.
4. Reexamination of the traditional major-minor syntax, effecting
   non-functional harmonic progression—i.e., progression and root
   movement *not* determined by a circle of fifths.

Claude Debussy's Sarabande from *Pour le Piano* (Example 289),
composed during the years 1896 to 1901, illustrates several of the
above influences. Anchored in the aesthetic of Impressionism, the
chordal structures remain tertian in their spelling and disposition;
yet the relationships from one chord to the next approach a return to
non-functional harmonic movement. Although an harmonic
analysis may be devised, the results do not seem altogether germaine.
For example, measures 1–2 would read:

In c♯ minor and modal:

$$\text{ii}^{\circ 7} \quad \text{iv}^7 \quad \natural\text{VII}^4_2 \quad \text{iv}^7 \quad \text{ii}^{\circ 7} \mid \text{III} \quad \text{v} \quad \text{v} \mid$$

The chord-to-chord progression seems to be determined by means
of *parallelism* or *planning*—generated from the opening sonority.
Debussy's parallel harmony and Medieval organum would appear
to share a common denominator. One may also speculate (see
observations below) that the opening chord defines the tonal structure
of this excerpt.

Observations:

1. Although Debussy's harmonic progressions appear to be non-
   functional in a chord to chord relationship, the chords do relate,
   and function, in a larger time-span. A middle-ground, or second
   harmonic dimension, analysis is given in Example 290.
2. Consider most carefully the organizing progression
   $$\text{ii}^7 \qquad \text{v (minor)} \qquad \text{i}$$
3. The aeolian mode is used for both melodic and harmonic formations.
4. The avoidance of the raised leading tone (minor dominant) is
   observed quite frequently in Impressionist music.
5. The whole-tone scale appears in measures 12–13: d e f♯ g♯ a♯ (in
   the bass line).

6. These 22 measures form a small ternary: a b a′. (Compare measure 19 to measure 5.) The excerpt, in turn, is the A section of a larger tri-partite design.

Example 289

Sarabande from *Pour le Piano*, Claude Debussy (1862–1918)

Example 290

Example 291

Canope from *Preludes, deuxieme livre,* Claude Debussy

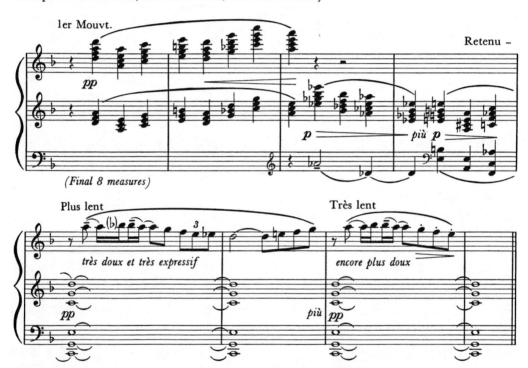

© 1913 Durand et Cie. Used by permission. Elkan-Vogel, Inc. sole representative in U.S.A.

Modal parallelism, abrupt tonal shifts, fluid rhythms, and open fifth sonorities are eloquently fused in this short composition (Example 291), entitled *Canope* (*Second Book of Preludes*). Of particular interest is measure 3, in which a shift to the flat side takes place without benefit (or perhaps distraction) of a modulation formula. Rather, a tri-tone relates the a minor triad to the eb minor triad, while the bass line assumes a temporary independent role. The *color* of sonorities held a special fascination for the Impressionist composers; and the relationships between painting, poetry, and music during this era are particularly striking.

ADDED TONE TECHNIQUE

The technique of adding a second, fourth, or sixth to a basic triad offers additional color resources in music. Usually referred to as the *added tone technique*, this additive process is commonly associated with the Impressionist composers. Appearances occur much earlier, however, and the tendency of late nineteenth-century composers to leave *appoggiature* and suspensions unresolved is a closely allied compositional technique. Example 292 illustrates the most basic formations.

Example 292

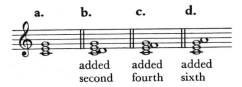

a.	b.	c.	d.
	added second	added fourth	added sixth

It is immediately apparent that these sonorities might be subjected to two or more views of analysis. Why is Example 292b not a ninth chord, 292c an eleventh chord, and 292d either a thirteenth chord or the first inversion of a seventh chord with A as its root? Most analytical judgements must be based on style, context, function, and chordal disposition. A few subjective analyses are provided below.

Example 293

a. Schumann: "dissolved" dissonance   **b.** Debussy: "added-tone" technique   **c.** J. S. Bach chordal seventh   **d.** Added sixth   **e.** Dominant thirteenth

Impressionist composers addressed themselves to the question of texture, color, and vertical spacing with particular adroitness. An excerpt from the first movement of Ravel's *String Quartet in F* illustrates how striking and luminous a d minor triad (with ninth) can sound. The first violin line is "registered" two octaves below in the viola (a technique Ravel probably discovered in the scores of Mozart). This spacious melodic scoring is stabilized by the harmonic and textural tremolos of the second violin. And, not least, the pizzicato cello buoys, punctuates, and provides harmonic clarification for the upper voices.

Example 294

Excerpt from first movement (second tonal area), *Quartet in F,*
Maurice Ravel (1873–1937)

1. Make a basic structural analysis of a short Impressionistic piano composition (see Debussy: *Preludes*, Books I,II). Comment on techniques used, scale resources, harmonic dispositions, and treatment of color and texture.
2. Using Debussy's *Canope* (Example 291) as a point of departure, write a short composition of about 20 measures for piano, in a similar style.
3. Using the following fragment (Example 295), compose a short piece for solo flute (or similar instrument) which continues with modal and whole-tone scale interplay.

Example 295

4. Using primary and secondary sources, write a short expository paper discussing the relationships between Impressionist painting, poetry, and music.

27

RHYTHM

COLOR AND TIMBRE

TEXTURE AND DENSITY

ORCHESTRATION

FORM

The first half of the twentieth century witnessed numerous changes in the inherited systems of Western music. Some innovations served as further expansions or modifications of the existing major-minor-tonal system; other developments, however, were antithetical to the conventions of the past and eventually produced a rethinking of the aesthetics and mechanics of music. Each parameter was scrutinized with a view to extracting its fullest potential. Rhythm, color, timbre, orchestration, texture, form—as well as melody and harmony—were each in turn used as the focal point of the composer's aural postulations.

RHYTHM

In the first decades of this century, a new rhythmic vitality was characteristic of many works. Syncopations, asymmetrical groupings, and free or rhapsodic rhythms are frequently observed. The question of durations was often coupled to the metric organization in a "war against the tyranny of the bar line." Such considerations led to several schemes of time organization, a few of which are cited below:

1. *Odd meters:* $\frac{5}{8}$ $\frac{7}{8}$ $\frac{11}{4}$

2. *Changing meters:* $\frac{2}{4}$ $\frac{3}{8}$ $\frac{3}{4}$ $\frac{1}{16}$ $\frac{5}{8}$

3. *Variable metrics—a predetermined scheme of metric organization:*
   $\frac{2}{8}$ $\frac{4}{8}$ $\frac{6}{8}$ $\frac{8}{8}$ $\frac{7}{8}$ $\frac{5}{8}$ $\frac{3}{8}$ (expansion by even meters and compression by odd meters)

4. *Metric modulation—a systematized change of rate and pulse:*
   $\frac{3}{8}$ ♪ = 60; ♪ = 80; ♪ = 100 $\frac{2}{4}$ ♩ = 60

236

Example 296

Excerpt from *Five Pieces for Orchestra,* Op. 16, III (*Farben*), Arnold
Schoenberg (1874–1951)

Reprinted from *Five Pieces for Orchestra* by Arnold Schoenberg, III—Summer Morning by a
Lake (Peters Nr. 6061). © 1952 by Henmar Press, Inc., New York. Reprint permission granted
by the publisher.

**COLOR
AND TIMBRE**

The possibilities of color and timbre were rather consistently explored by most composers. Two concepts are of particular importance—both of which may provide new life for a series of pitches.

1. *Klang farbenmelodie* literally means tone-color melody.
   A particularly striking passage is shown in Example 296.
2. *Pointillism* is a term borrowed from painting. It refers to *points* of color which collectively effect a representational or semi-representational likeness of the painter's subject matter. (See Examples 297, 322.)

In a facetious vein, the following example uses a well-known tune and subjects it to a free rhythmic arrangement, *octave displacement* (i.e., substitution of a different octave for the given note), and to a pointillistic treatment.

Example 297

Observations:

1. Points of instrumental color create a constantly changing texture. In viewing a pointillistic painting, one should stand at some distance in order to perceive the whole; similarly, one should "stand back" aurally in order to absorb the totality of pointillistic musical fabric.
2. The use of different orchestral timbres evokes a *tone-painting* of nearly infinite potential.

Queries:

1. What is the paraphrased melody?
2. Is the example within a given tonality?

**TEXTURE
AND DENSITY**

Texture is often a significant facet of composition, providing depth and dimension and contributing to the organization of time-span. Texture per se *may* be used as a form-producing parameter, especially in the control of density. The graphic notation in Example 14 conveys, among other aspects, the "thicks" and "thins" of texture.

**ORCHESTRA-
TION**

One of the most radical departures from previous practice can be observed in the instrumentation and orchestration that has been employed by twentieth-century composers. From among the numerous innovations, a few are cited:

1. A complete and independent use of our orchestral choirs: winds, brasses, percussion, and strings.
2. Scoring for special combinations of instruments such as thirteen diverse colors, or eight 'celli and voice.
3. The use of extended ranges and new sound potentials such as the "prepared" piano, stringed instruments bowed beyond the bridge, use of wind instrument mouthpieces.
4. The addition of diverse percussion and electronic instruments to the standard orchestral complement.

FORM

As with the "shape" of the universe, any discussion of musical form of this century is out of date before it has even been verbalized. Philosophy aside, the reader is advised to consider at least three principal categories for twentieth-century musical form:

1. Modifications of eighteenth- and nineteenth-century principles of musical design
2. Structural innovations and practices which relate specifically to the twentieth century.
3. Form which results quite inclusively from a sound-event series. In this category one must consider such items as improvisation, random and chance events, the "counterpoint of sound and silence," and noise in relationship to musical sound.

The principles of binary, ternary, sonata, rondo, and variation have been freely utilized by twentieth-century composers. These parent forms, however, have been modified substantially—particularly with regard to repetition. The psychological impact of sound and of experience from sound have been carefully considered. An hypothetical comparison will serve to illustrate:

Ternary principle (nineteenth-century):

A	B	A
16 measures	12–16 measures	exact repetition

Ternary principle (twentieth-century):

A	B	A'/(B)
15 measures	11 measures	13 measures comprised of short quotations from A and B; possibly in inverted or retrograde form.

Some writers refer to this twentieth-century foreshortening of the repeated portions as *dynamic symmetry*—a symmetry resulting from the weight of musical event and experience rather than from a symmetrical proportioning of the time-span.

Arch forms, wedge-shaped designs, and cantilever constructions have been employed with considerable frequency by twentieth-century composers.

Arch: 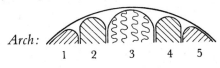 Sections 1 and 5 related; 2 and 4 related; 3 independent

Wedge: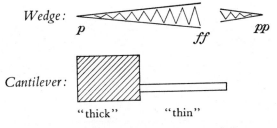

Cantilever: "thick"   "thin"

Aleatory (L. *aleatorius* and Fr. *alea*, chance, hazard, risk) and *free improvisation* in music veer from the traditionally accepted attitudes regarding form and the purposes of form. Perhaps one could venture the observation that form which results from a fully notated composition considers the physiological and psychological consequences of structure, whereas aleatoric composition addresses itself to the philosophical significance of the time-continuum.

SUGGESTED
STUDIES

1. Suggested reading:
   Leon Dallin, *Techniques of Twentieth Century Harmony* (Dubuque, Iowa: Wm. C. Brown Company Publishers, 1957)
   Allen Forte, *Contemporary Tone-Structures* (New York: Columbia University Press, 1955)
   G. Welton Marquis, *Twentieth Century Music Idioms* (Englewood Cliffs, N.J.: Prentice-Hall, 1964)
   Vincent Persichetti, *Twentieth Century Harmony* (New York: W. W. Norton Company, 1961)

2. Write a short composition for percussion instruments (or sound-producing objects) in which variable metrics and a wedge design are employed.

3. Paraphrase a familiar folk song for four or five different instruments, employing the techniques of octave displacement and pointillism.

4. Using the excerpt from the song *Serenity* by Charles Ives (Example

298), prepare an analysis providing three of four points on each
of the following: harmony, melody, rhythm/meter, structure/
repetition, texture/dynamics.

Example 298

*Serenity,** Charles Ives (1874–1954)

John G. Whittier (1807–1892)

Copyright 1942, 1969 by Associated Music Publishers, Inc., New York. All rights reserved
including the right of public performance for profit. Used by permission.

* About 1919, according to the Catalogue of Ives Manuscripts, compiled by John Kirkpatrick.

28

QUARTAL HARMONY

ANALYTICAL SYSTEM (HINDEMITH)

PANDIATONICISM

In Western music, vertical sonorities are produced primarily by three different kinds of harmony:

Secundal: spelling of chords in intervals of seconds
Tertian: spelling of chords in thirds
Quartal: spelling of chords in fourths

All other spellings are formed from interval inversion, and there exists a modest debate among writers as to whether these three kinds of harmony coexist or are, rather, mutually interchangeable. Example 299 illustrates:

Example 299

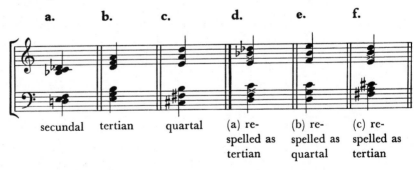

| a. | b. | c. | d. | e. | f. |

secundal   tertian   quartal   (a) re-   (b) re-   (c) re-
                                  spelled as spelled as spelled as
                                  tertian   quartal   tertian

QUARTAL HARMONY

Paul Hindemith's chanson *Since all is passing* (Example 300) provides an excellent example of combined tertian-quartal harmony. The interplay produces a fresh and appealing sonority within a tonal and traditional framework.

Observations:

1. Deliberate quartal (or the inverted, quintal) dispositions are to be found in each of the 17 measures.
2. Parallel perfect fourths or perfect fifths provide for open, quasi-archaic sonorities.
3. The composition has a tonal orientation to G, although chord-to-chord progressions are non-functional in the traditional sense.
4. Cadences are exceptionally clear: on B, G, C, G—achieving internal variety; the cadences are typically approached by a strong bass line which ascends or descends diatonically.
5. The four phrases (a b c b) contain only one non-symmetrical feature—that of the elongation of the third phrase.

Example 300

Since all is passing, Paul Hindemith (1895–1963)

Rainer Maria Rilke
English version by Elaine de Sinçay

**ANALYTICAL
SYSTEM
(Hindemith)**

Hindemith set forth his analytical concepts in Volume I of *The Craft
of Musical Composition: Theory*. He attempted to reach a system of
analysis which could accurately describe the root of any chord
(however complex), harmonic value, strength and fluctuation, and
tonality at any given moment. His many suggestions included the
following:

1. Construction in thirds should no longer be the basic rule for
   erection of chords.
2. An all-embracing principle should be substituted for the description of chordal invertibility.
3. The thesis that chords are susceptible to a variety of interpretations
   should be abandoned.

Hindemith classified all chords into two groups: *Group A:* chords
without a tritone; *Group B:* chords containing a tritone. Group A
is further divided into two series: 1. melodic, and 2. harmonic,
according to the relationship to the "progenitor tone."

Example 301

Series 1:

Series 2:

Hindemith also suggests that for both series the fifths, fourths,
thirds, and sixths are "first-generation descendants" of the progenitor
tone (the tone C in the example above), while seconds and sevenths
form a "second-generation" relationship.

Although disputed by some theorists, Hindemith's concepts contain valuable insight into melodic (intervallic) relationships as well as
harmonic function and determination of roots. Of special interest is
his *Table of Chord Groups*, which prescribes the method of determining chord roots. Best intervals and roots of selected chords are shown
in Example 302.

Example 302

Chord:

Best interval:

Root:

**PANDIATONIC-
ISM**

A vocabulary used extensively by American and French composers in the second and third decades of this century consisted of a linearly conceived, non-functional diatonicism. Sometimes referred to as "white-key music," it is perhaps more aptly termed *pandiatonicism* (i.e., an all-inclusive, essentially non-chromatic pitch series). Often, one or more of the convergent lines will suggest a mode, freely employed. Phrygian, dorian, and aeolian characteristics seem to have been particularly popular.

The independence of each line, within the tonal/modal restrictions set by the composer, can scarcely be overemphasized. The linear process contributes to the non-functionalism of chords. As a result, modulation in the traditional sense is unnecessary—since a freedom of tonal orientation and of cadence already exists. To illustrate, the cadence in measure 6 of Stravinsky's *Dithyrambe* (Example 303a) is shown rewritten four times (303b–e)—not as improvements, but as possible alternatives within the style:

Example 303

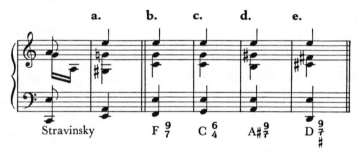

Example 304

Dithyrambe, Igor Stravinsky (1882–1971)

Observations:

1. Stravinsky's structure of *Dithyrambe* (Example 304) suggests more than a simple ABA. The A sections serve as introduction and conclusion and "frame" to the middle section, which in turn is divided into two parts: B1, the expansive, unmeasured *parlando*; followed by B2, the chordal focal point and climax.

2. The tonal orientation is to C, with a tritone relationship to the climax.

3. Except for the chordal climax, the texture moves freely from four to six voices, including the solo violin. Control of range and of register create the movement's dramatic shape.

4. Examination of the vertical sonorities reveals an expanded tertian vocabulary. As a typical sampling, chord structures *a* through *e* (the latter, see analysis below, certainly the most ambiguous of these five chords) on the second page of the example would seem to indicate the absence of a systematized root movement.

$$\text{a. } F_9^{11} \quad \text{b. } C_9^{11} \quad \text{c. } D_9^{13} \quad \text{d. } C^7 \quad \text{e. } D_{+6}^9$$
$$\quad\;\; 7 \qquad\qquad\;\; 7$$

SUGGESTED STUDIES

1. Compose a short (about 21–28 measures) composition which incorporates the following passage of tertian-quartal harmonic counterpoint:

Example 305

2. Determine the chord roots of Hindemith's *Since all is passing* (Example 300) by consulting the composer's *Table of Chord-Groups* (p. 247). Be prepared to discuss the following questions:
   a. Does the information on chord roots assist in understanding the harmonic structure of the composition?
   b. What are the areas of agreement and disagreement between Hindemith's system and traditional root analysis?

3. As an experiment, continue the five-voice fragment in Example 306 for an additional nine measures. Use no accidentals; write one line at a time, considering the contour and musicality of each line. Cover each completed line before writing a new voice. After all five voices are completed, play or perform the total composition. Carefully study the pandiatonic, non-functional results.

Example 306

4. Write a short composition with the following requirements:
   Piano, four hands
   Phrygian or dorian characteristics (essentially white key)
   Phrase design: A (9 measures), B (7 measures), A′ (5 measures)

5. Analyze and perform the following excerpts from Stravinsky's *Ave Maria* (Example 307). Study the contour of each line, the vertical coincidence, and the cadence practice.

Example 307

Excerpts from *Ave Maria*, Igor Stravinsky

b.

nunc   et in   ho - ra mor - tis   nos - trae.   A - men.

nunc   et in   ho - ra mor - tis   nos - trae.   A - men.

nunc   et in   ho - ra mor - tis   nos - trae.   A - men.

nunc   et in   ho - ra mor - tis   nos - trae.   A - men.

29

SYNTHETIC SCALES

MELODIC METAMORPHOSIS

HARMONIC RESOURCES OF THE

TERTIAN SYSTEM

SYNTHETIC SCALES

Synthetic scales of all varieties have either formed or complemented the pitch materials of numerous twentieth-century compositions. It is presumed, theoretically, that three different pitches are sufficient to qualify as a *scale*—hence, the possibilities are abundant, even within the equal temperament octave. An excellent example of scale employ-ment and development is observed in Walter Piston's expressive *Passacaglia* (Example 309). The passacaglia theme, or "ground," may perhaps be considered derivative from a scale formed by two slightly asymmetrical tetrachords. Obviously, the scale is freely deployed and represents a reduction of the "theme." A reduction of each four-measure section reveals a most interesting scalar evolution or meta-morphosis. Example 308 illustrates:

Example 308

a. Reduction of theme

b. Version I: measures 1–4 (upper voice)

c. Version II: measures 5–8

d. Version III: measures 9–12

e. Version IV: measures 13–16

Example 309

From *Passacaglia*, Walter Piston (1895–   )

Observations:

1. The gradual introduction of chromaticism subtly effects a musical tension.
2. The 5/8 meter provides for a rhythmic asymmetry; the phrase overlaps cover the structural seams.
3. Changes in register (range) and texture secure a logical unfolding of these continuous variations.

Queries:

1. What similarities and differences are observed between this passacaglia and an eighteenth-century passacaglia?
2. Could the first four measures constitute the beginnings of a chaconne?

Béla Bartók's sophisticated *Children's Song* from the *Mikrokosmos* is quoted in its entirety (Example 310). The 44 measures constitute a consummate study in the control of line and motive, modal combinations, phrase expansion, and arch form.

Observations:

1. Bartók's arch structure in *Children's Song* (Example 310) is as follows:

Designation:	A	B	A′	B′	A″
Measures:	1–8	9–18	19–26	27–36	37–44
Number of bars:	8	10	8	10	8

2. The composition seems to be derived from two forms of a single motive which appears in measures 1–2.
3. Interest is achieved by the interaction of opposing tetrachords. For example, measures 1–8, left hand: the upper tetrachord from A melodic minor (or major) opposes a dorian tetrachord centered on D.
4. Measures 9–10, right hand, illustrate a melodic variant of measures 1–2, right hand.
5. Measures 19–26 are the transposed, inverted, and modified version of measures 1–8.
6. Measures 27–36 invert and modify measures 9–18.
7. Measures 37–44 present the final version of measures 1–8.
8. The basic harmonic/tonal structure may be diagrammed as in Example 311.

Observe that the analysis in Example 311 shows a tonal orientation to F♯, which is surrounded by thirds and leading tones. V through Z represents perhaps a chromatic ascension to an emphatic tonic.

Example 310

Children's Song, Mikrokosmos, Vol. IV, No. 106, Béla Bartók
(1881–1945)

Example 311

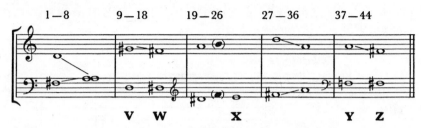

**MELODIC
METAMOR-
PHOSIS**

The gradual change of a motive or theme is commonly referred to as *melodic metamorphosis*. Modifications of the original may include the devices of mirror, retrograde, augmentation, diminution, as well as transposition, interval expansion or contraction, truncation or fragmentation of themes and/or rhythms, and the successive transformation of the original interval series. In short, the process of melodic metamorphosis is limited only by the composer's imagination.

A synthetic scale which alternates half-steps with whole-steps (previously quoted in Example 18) is employed in Example 312 to further illustrate melodic metamorphosis as well as its harmonic use.

Example 312

a. Basic synthetic scale

b. Melody derived from scale

c. Retrograde, inversion, transposed; slight rhythmic and intervallic changes

d. Inversion, augmentation, transposed, interval repetition

e. Used vertically, the same scale achieves new harmonic possibilities. (The F♮ is extraneous to the scale.)

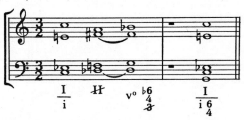

**HARMONIC
RESOURCES
OF THE
TERTIAN
SYSTEM**

In several respects, the tertian harmonic system "reached the ceiling" (to borrow Olivier Messiaen's phrase) in the first half of the twentieth century. One may counter, however, that the possible combinations of the basic system are nearly inexhaustible—particularly when coupled to the resources of color and timbre, disposition, dynamics, and articulation. Arnold Schoenberg purportedly stated that there were still beautiful C major triads to be written. The following displacement of C E G is not an attempt to heed this admonition, but the scoring may suggest to the reader some perception of musical infinity.

Example 313

six violins, unison, harmonics, *ppp*

vibraphone, one alto flute, *ppp*

harp, four double basses, unison, *ppp*

"Displaced" bass

In addition to scoring and pitch disposition, other items should be mentioned which further the harmonic resources of the tertian system. These would include:

1. *"Displaced bass"*
2. Bi-chordal and polychordal formations
3. Expansions beyond the thirteenth chord to twelve-note chords
4. Expansion of clusters to the extent that each instrument plays a different note

An independent, or even "displaced," bass line is observed with some frequency in twentieth-century music. Two examples are shown (Example 314):

Example 314

a. Invented. The bass
line of I IV V I
in C major has moved
down a whole step,
hence the term
"displacement."

b. *Sacre du Printemps,*
by Stravinsky.
Parallel MM
seventh chords
are countered by
a seemingly
"independent"
bass line.

Polytonality

Numerous twentieth-century composers have experimented
with *bi-tonality* (two independent tonal centers functioning
simultaneously) or with *polytonality* (several simultaneous tonalities).
Multiple key signatures sometimes have been used to show the
composer's intent; on other occasions no signatures have been
used—rather, the individual accidentals provided the necessary
information.

Example 315

a. Prokofiev   **b.** Bartók   **c.** Milhaud

If Example 315c continued to function at the levels of F, G, and A,
the resultant would be *polytonal*. With the information given,
however, the example should accurately be termed *polychordal*. The
superimposition of chords a perfect fifth apart was considerably in
vogue in the third and fourth decades of this century—particularly in
French and American scores. There are obviously solid acoustical
factors which support this interesting sonority, as Example 316
shows:

Example 316

**Twelve-note
chords**

Beyond the thirteenth chords lies a chromatic area of fifteenth, seventeenth, nineteenth, twenty-first, twenty-third chords. The author and reader will happily and mutually acknowledge that the "twenty-third chord" represents the limit of the tertian system in this particular theoretical sense. It is observed that, with all twelve tones utilized, additions simply result in unison or octave equivalents.

Example 317

Tone clusters

Disposition of pitches into *tone clusters* in twentieth-century music merits special consideration. Not infrequently, clusters have been comprised of tertian formations plus two or more added tones—resulting, of course, in blurred sonorities. Interestingly enough, the cluster was not devised in the twentieth century. Eighteenth-century examples are observed in the keyboard works of Domenico Scarlatti and, less boldly, in the A minor Piano Sonata of Mozart. An extraordinary example comes from Michel Corrette (1709-1795), a French composer who called for "thunder" to be produced on the organ by using a board which depressed several pedal tones simultaneously. In the twentieth century, Henry Cowell, Charles Ives, Béla Bartók, and more recently Krzysztof Penderecki, among numerous others, have explored the quite unique sound of closely-spaced tones. The following fragment of Bartók's *Melody in the Mist,* Mikrokosmos (Example 318) illustrates a possible use of tone clusters.

Example 318

Melody in the Mist, Mikrokosmos, Vol. IV, No. 107, Béla Bartók

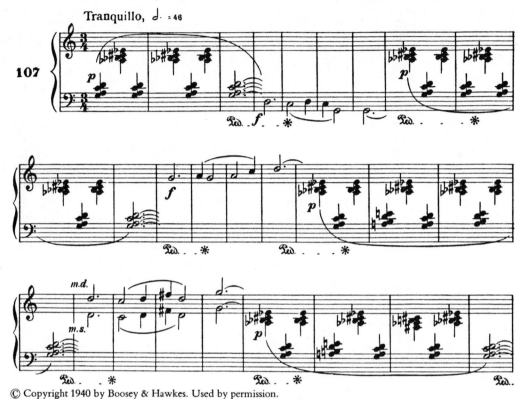

SUGGESTED STUDIES

1. Make an independent analysis of at least one additional composition from the Mikrokosmos, Volumes IV, V, or VI.
2. Write a short composition (about 28 measures) for solo clarinet or similar instrument, using a synthetic scale and the process of melodic metamorphosis.
3. Write a consequent section to the two-voice incomplete composition in Example 319.

Example 319

30

TWELVE-TONE METHOD

PANTONALITY

PERMUTATION

CANON CANCRIZANS

In architecture, expansion in height necessitates special building principles or materials. The pyramids of Egypt and, later, the temples of Greece and the Roman domes required interlocking, broadly-based support; the flying buttress concept made possible the lofty Medieval cathedrals; the Empire State Building is a reality because of the combined strengths of steel and concrete.

Similarly in music, expansion of a system requires a rethinking of the basic principles involved; new methods or materials are perhaps needed to serve as substitutes for the established ones; or perhaps an altogether new system has to be devised to replace the old system which seems to be in disarray.

TWELVE-TONE METHOD

Of the several attempts made in this century to find viable alternatives to the overly extended major-minor-tonal system, none has been more influential and controversial than Arnold Schoenberg's "method of composing with twelve tones." Schoenberg and others viewed with concern the tonal system they considered extended to its limits and capable of no further significant growth. In a desire to restabilize pitch materials of composition, Schoenberg suggested certain methods and procedures. A few of these procedures are paraphrased and interpreted below:

1. The twelve tones of the equal-tempered octave should contribute independently and as equally as possible to the musical structure and fabric.
2. The pitch resources of each composition (or movement) are to reside in a *tone row* or *series* which employs all twelve tones. The row is invented by the composer at a pre-compositional stage.

264

(This process is not too dissimilar to the invention of a synthetic scale, used as a basis for melodic and harmonic vocabulary.)

3. Any series (row) has four forms, each of which is capable of eleven transpositions.

   a. Original row (O)
   b. Retrograde (R)
   c. Inversion (I), also called "mirror"
   d. Retrograde Inversion (RI)

A chart of transpositions or *matrix* (see p. 267) will provide 48 different versions of the basic row. As an example, if the first three notes of a row (original form) are A B♭ G, then the first transposition would be A♯ B♮ G♯, the second transposition B♭ C♮ A♮, etc.—ascending chromatically through eleven transpositions.

4. Certain considerations regarding the makeup of the series were postulated—and subsequently modified. These included:

   a. Avoidance of a return to a note of the series prior to the complete unfolding of the row form
   b. Avoidance in the series of triadic outlines which might produce unintended tonal implications
   c. Enharmonic equivalents as well as octave displacements were to be considered, in a theoretical sense, as identical to the original note of the series

A row obviously gives clues to a particular composer's selective processes. Compare, for example, the following rows:

Example 320

a. *String Quartet*, Op. 28, Anton Webern (1883-1945)

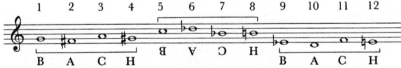

b. *Concerto for Violin and Orchestra*, Alban Berg (1885-1935)

c. *Structures I*, for two pianos, Pierre Boulez (1925-   )

d. *Edge of Shadow*, for chorus and instruments, Ross Lee Finney
(1906–   )

e. *Quaderno di Anna Libera*, for piano, Luigi Dallapiccola (1904–   )

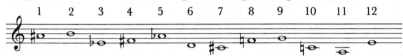

It is observed that a row may be comprised of quasi-motivic trichords or tetrachords (three-note or four-note groupings), or divided as two symmetrical hexachords; it may be expansive—with a range of several octaves; it may be, in itself, melodically germinating, approaching what was traditionally called a *theme*.

PANTONALITY   Obviously, the *employment* of serial techniques is both personal and individual. Rows may be used to produce explicit tonalities, or the tonal orientation may be vaguely suggested. Finally, the seeming absence of any central or principal tonal center produces what is perhaps best termed *pantonality* (i.e., all-encompassing and variable tonal orientations which, in turn, prescribe their own larger dimension).

Three twelve-tone analyses are offered on the following pages as an introduction to serial methods.[1]

Ross Lee Finney's symmetrical hexachords (see Example 320d) are manipulated to produce strongly tonal and functional choral parts in *Edge of Shadow*. In the following excerpt (Example 321), the instrumental parts are omitted.

Observations:

1. The simultaneous use of two transpositions of the row, a perfect fifth apart, allows for a flexible treatment and manipulation.
2. The homophonic texture and the repeated pitches provide for stability and a kind of instantaneous familiarity.
3. The slow harmonic rhythm results from *prolongation* (i.e., extension in time caused by the setting of the text).
4. The passage relates in several ways to certain aspects of the "familiar style" of the sixteenth century, yet the totality (including the instrumental accompaniment) is decidedly, and lyrically, of this century.

[1] There are two principal ways of numbering serialized pitch: 1 through 12 and 0 through 11. 1–12 is used in most introductory discussions; 0–11 is appropriate for mathematical considerations (mod 12). Each has advantages.

Example 321

Excerpt from *Edge of Shadow* (1959), Ross Lee Finney; text by Archibald MacLeish

Reprinted from *Edge of Shadow* by Ross Lee Finney (Peters Nr. 6192). © 1960 by Henmar Press, Inc., New York. Reprint permission granted by the publisher.

Matrix   A matrix, constructed from the Webern row (Example 320a), follows:

Inversion ↓

Original →	1	2	3	4	5	6	7	8	9	10	11	12	
1	G	F♯	A	G♯	C	D♭	B♭	B	E♭	D	F	E	← Retrograde
2	A♭	G	B♭	A	C♯	D	B	C	E	D♯	F♯	F	
3	F	E	G	F♯	B♭	B	G♯	A	C♯	C	D♯	D	
4	F♯	F	A♭	G	B	C	A	B♭	D	C♯	E	E♭	
5	D	C♯	E	D♯	G	A♭	F	F♯	B♭	A	C	B	
6	C♯	C	E♭	D	F♯	G	E	F	A	G♯	B	B♭	
7	E	E♭	F♯	F	A	B♭	G	A♭	C	B	D	D♭	
8	D♯	D	F	E	G♯	A	F♯	G	B	B♭	C♯	C	
9	B	B♭	C♯	C	E	F	D	D♯	G	F♯	A	G♯	
10	C	B	D	C♯	F	F♯	E♭	E	A♭	G	B♭	A	
11	A	G♯	B	B♭	D	E♭	C	C♯	F	E	G	F♯	
12	B♭	A	C	B	D♯	E	C♯	D	F♯	F	A♭	G	

↑
Retrograde inversion

Example 322

String Quartet, Op. 28, Anton Webern

Observations:

1. Because of the symmetry of the row, duplications result. As examples: O1 is identical to RI 12; O2 to RI 11, etc. Similarly, the row provides ample opportunity for "overlapping" technique (i.e., 9, 10, 11, 12 of one row-form will equal 1, 2, 3, 4 of a different form); also, 11, 12 of one form will be 1, 2 of a different form.

2. Webern's 15 measures (Example 322) constitute a "theme area" after which a set of variations follows.

3. Phrase and period equivalents are seemingly defined by a function in time—i.e., *rests*—rather than by harmonic or melodic function.

4. Timbre, color, and register are explored within a constantly shifting one- and two-voice texture.

5. A reduction, without octave displacements (Example 323), reveals a most fascinating relationship to tradition—one is tempted to suggest that a certain spirit of the Renaissance exists in the music.

Example 323

Since the mid-1920's, when serial techniques were initiated, numerous modifications and extensions of the original rationale have been made. A few of the modifications will serve to illustrate:

PERMUTATION

1. *Row permutation,* e.g.:
   1 3 5 7 9 11 12 10 8 6 4 2 of the original effects a new but related row.

2. *Use of hexachords or partial series* rather than twelve-tone series.

3. *Total serialization*—i.e., serial techniques applied to the parameters of pitch, duration, dynamic, articulation, etc.

4. *Free use.* There exists a large number of compositions in which serial methods were probably used at an early or pre-compositional stage, but which in the eventual course of "working out" became so modified that a strict, note-by-note analysis would be futile.

CANON CANCRIZANS

Luigi Dallapiccola's *Quaderno di Anna Libera* (*The Notebook of Anna Libera*) is a set of eleven short pieces for piano based on a single row. The entire composition is further unified by traditional means of contrast and repetition of kind (i.e., types of texture, devices, structure). Dallapiccola's lyric and "thematic" treatment of serial methods serves to illustrate the procedure's flexibility. Number 7 of the *Quaderno* is a movement of singular beauty and amazing technical accomplishment. This canon cancrizans is quoted in Example 324.

Example 324

From *Quaderno di Anna Libera*, Luigi Dallapiccola
N.7 – ANDANTINO AMOROSO E CONTRAPUNCTUS TERTIUS (CANON CANCRIZANS)

1 min.

Observations:

1. The row of the *Quaderno* was previously stated (Example 320e).
2. The fact that serial techniques and polyphonic devices are employed in no way precludes the use of tertian formations—which are in considerable evidence.
3. There seems to be an elusive yet implied tonal orientation and a suggested function in this canon. Example 325 illustrates:

Example 325

tonic implication   dominant implication   tonic

4. Dallapiccola's *Quaderno* also exists in an orchestral version made by the composer: *Variations for Orchestra*, to which the reader is directed for further insight into the expressive twentieth century.

SUGGESTED
STUDIES

1. Complete a row analysis of any of the other movements from the *Quaderno*. In addition, study the bi-partite and tri-partite structures, tertian formations, melodic writing, contrapuntal devices employed, and the implied broad tonal orientations.
2. Compose a set of miniatures for string quartet, using serial methods and pointillistic techniques.
3. Compose a short song or piano piece in which the row is thematic.
4. Suggested reading:
   George Perle: *Serial Composition and Atonality*, 3rd ed. (Berkeley: The University of California Press, 1972)

POSTSCRIPT

To conclude a theory text with an example of a contemporary canon cancrizans suggests perhaps that the reader should reread the text backward and forward. The same results might be achieved more naturally by undertaking a series of "vertical" reviews such as those suggested:

1. A study of cell, figure, and motive from chant to the twentieth century
2. A study of tonal orientation from the Renaissance to the present
3. A study of variation principles as used by sixteenth-, eighteenth-, and twentieth-century composers.
4. A study of *cantus firmus* techniques as observed from the fifteenth century to the present

It is further suggested that study of complete compositions be made. These scores might include: Josquin's motet: *Ave Maria*; J. S. Bach's *Cantata No. 4*; Haydn's *Symphony No. 104*; the Chopin *Preludes*, Op. 28; Ravel's *Ma mere l'oye*; Stravinsky's *In Memoriam Dylan Thomas*; Dallapiccola's complete *Quaderno di Anna Libera*; and a score in newer notation, such as Penderecki's *Threnody for 52 Strings*.

Living in an age of technology during a century of transition is often difficult for the poet, painter, and musician. Individual personal and professional roles are seldom well-defined; the purpose and function of the arts seem diffuse and inundated by the social events of history; societies appear to grant little priority to civilizing endeavors. Cultures become vital, however, and subsequently admired and emulated, by the degree of progress of the spirit. It is in this realm that the study of music may be engaged with confidence. Mankind will hopefully always seek the enjoyment, inspiration, and solace which Music, as an extension of reality, provides.

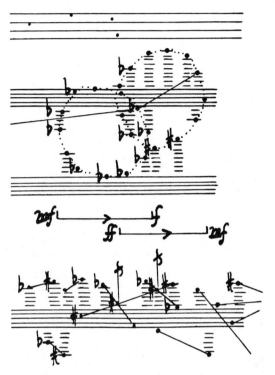

Fragment from *Concert for Piano and Orchestra* (*Solo for Piano*) by John Cage. © 1960 by Henmar Press, Inc., New York. Reprint permission granted by the publishers.

*"Teachers open the door. . . . You enter by
yourself."*

—Ancient Chinese Proverb

INDEX